CANADIAN ORDERS, DECORATIONS and MEDALS
3rd Edition

by Surgeon Commander F.J. Blatherwick, C.D.

THE UNITRADE PRESS
TORONTO

Copyright© 1985 by The Unitrade Press

Printed and Bound in Canada.

Production Editor: Don Wainwright.

Typesetting by Mastertype, Toronto.

Canadian Cataloguing in Publication Data

Blatherwick, F.J. (Francis John), 1944-
Canadian orders, decorations and medals

ISBN 0-919801-21-8

1. Medals - Canada.   2. Decorations of honour - Canada.
I. Title.

CJ5826.B52 1984   737'.223'0971   C84-098987-3

THE UNITRADE PRESS
TORONTO

The Unitrade Press - P.O. Box 172, Station A Toronto, Ontario M5W 1B2
Telephone (416) 787-5658   Telex 09-969719

TABLE OF CONTENTS

Page

INTRODUCTION

This is the third publishing of this book, one a limited edition by the author and the second a professionally done production by the Unitrade Press. Don Wainwright of Unitrade has been extremely helpful in ensuring the success of this book. There are a multitude of changes in this edition from the original two and while I cannot claim that this is the definitive work on Canadian medals, it certainly is a great improvement on the previous books. When Unitrade published the book in 1983, one would not have expected a country with so few medals to establish four new medals in 1984. However, 1984 saw the Police Exemplary Service Medal, Corrections Exemplary Service Medal, Meritorious Service Cross and Special Service Medal established. These are all covered in this book.

In 1969, Mr. Ross W. Irwin printed a book "War Medals and Decorations of Canada". This book is patterned after that book and Mr. Irwin has been very kind to allow me to use much of the research that went into that book. LCol. (ret.) N.A. Buchingham, Director of Ceremonial, Department of National Defence assisted in bringing the current medal information up to date.

Mr. David John, Deputy Director of the Chancellery of Canadian Orders and Decorations, has helped greatly in the update of this book. The Chancellery would like Canadians to be made aware of the system of official Canadian Government Awards system and to make the distinction between official, semi-official and unofficial awards.

A) OFFICIAL:
Those honours that emanate from the Sovereign and are created and modified by Royal Warrant of Letters Patent signed by the Sovereign are official awards. These also include United Nations and Truce Commission Medals accepted for wear by Canadians by Order in Council. Ribbons and non-neck-badge insignia are worn on the left breast in the sequence approved by Order in Council and published by the Chancellery. The term official also applies to foreign honours emanating from a head of state, the award of which to Canadians is approved by the Canadian Government and published in the Canada Gazette. Such honours may be worn with official Canadian insignia in the approved sequence as noted in this book.

B) SEMI-OFFICIAL:
They are actually unofficial but have the approbation of the Sovereign. The life-saving medals of the Royal Humane Society and the Royal Canadian Humane Association and the Life Saving Medal of the Order of St. John are the only ones authorized to be worn on the right breast.

C) UNOFFICIAL:
Every other award is an unofficial award. All of the provincial awards and all societal awards fall into this category. None of them have any official status except to the Province or society awarding them and therefore should **never** be worn with official insignia. Examples of these awards include the Ontario Provincial Police Long Service and Good Conduct Medal, the Ontario Fire Services Long Service Medal, Canadian

Banks Law Enforcement Award, British Columbia Corps of Commissionaires Long Service Award and their Meritorious Service Medal and the Canadian Corps of Commissionaires Long Service Medal which were described in the earlier edition of this book but have been omitted from this edition. The Canadian Association of Chiefs of Police Service Medal has been superceded by the official Police Exemplary Service Medal and therefore is omitted from this book. Despite the authors love of aviation, the Canadian Aviation Awards have also been omitted.

Thus in updating this book, I have concentrated solely on official awards, Canadian and British. For those people with the previous books, the Royal Victorian Order has been extensively updated and the Queen's Medal for the Champion Shots have been corrected. The quantity of medals given in a number of awards have been corrected to reflect the current research and these changes occur throughout the book.

One other point from the Canadian Chancellery of Orders and Decorations is that the insignia of the Order of Canada and the Order of Military Merit are the property of the Order. The Chancellery has no intention of recovering those pieces that pass legitimately from the deceased recipient's estate into collector's hands but will recover stolen items. Collectors should check with the Chancellery (Rideau Hall, Ottawa, Ontario, K1A 0A1) on the legitimacy of a prospective sale. They will also provide information (recipient, date of award, citation) on each piece for the collector.

MEDAL PRICES

The prices listed are for single medals, usually unnamed in very fine condition. The prices listed are those prices asked by the major Canadian dealers for these medals. Price values vary especially with named medals depending on the rank, regiment and scarcity of the medal. Bravery medals in a group generally go for two to three times as much as the unnamed equivalent. A DFC in case of issue, unnamed sells for $600.00 but in a group with a named long service medal it sells for $1200.00. The Order of Canada medals reflect the prices paid at a recent auction. In the case of the Companion of the Order of Canada Medal to M.J. Caldwell, the family sold it to a dealer for $1500.00 and it sold at auction for $9298 (1982).

Many medals issued to Canadians are identical to British medals. I have thus listed the prices of British medals being sold in Canada. The collector must decide if it is worth $400.00 for an RCAF Long Service Medal because it is named to a Canadian or if the identical medal named to an RAF member would not suffice at $75.00. I have also listed the existence of copies that I have come across to warn collectors as some are excellent copies. The unnamed specimen medals also represent a method of purchasing expensive medals for reasonable prices. The prices for miniatures is included as purchasing miniatures is a good way to collect the expensive Orders and Decorations. Prices in miniatures vary greatly depending on quality so beware of the very cheap miniatures and shop around for the very expensive ones.

The common medals have reduced in price over the past three years and should continue to fall with the devalued British Pound. However, collecting has grown considerably in this period and valuable pieces (named bravery decorations) have held their own in price and even increased. The prices listed at the end of this book are only a guide and represent the prices asked for by Canadian dealers in early 1985. Prices that are considerably lower may be due to the condition of the medal and prices that are considerably higher may have to do with the rank or regiment of that particular medal. It is best to deal with established dealers especially when purchasing an expensive medal.

CLUBS

The Canadian Society of Military Medals and Insignia — 1985 dues $10.00 c/o Club Secretary, 15 Greenhill Drive, THOROLD, Ontario, L2V 1W4

The Military Collectors Club of Canada — 1985 dues $20.00 c/o Club Secretary, 15 Abel Place, St. Albert, Alberta T8N 2Z5

Both produce Journals and Newsletters, exchanges and Canadian Dealers advertisements.

Dedicated to my wife Carol Elaine Blatherwick and my three sons:
James Edward Blatherwick
David Allan Blatherwick
Douglas Stephen Blatherwick

John Blatherwick
August 1985

AUTHOR:

Surgeon Commander Francis John Blatherwick, CD, BSC, DPH, MD, FRCP (C). Dr. Blatherwick is the Medical Health Officer of the City of Vancouver in civilian life and the Principal Medical Officer of the Naval Reserve Unit in Vancouver, HMCS Discovery. He has served in the Canadian Forces since 1961 with the Governor General's Foot Guards, the Royal Canadian Air Force (418 Squadron), the Royal Canadian Army Medical Corps and joined the Royal Canadian Navy Reserves in 1971. He has written five previous books and Unitrade will be publishing his next book 'Canadian Airline Histories' in late 1985. Comments on improving this book are welcome and should be sent to the author at 1060 West 8th Avenue, Vancouver, B.C. V6H 1C4.

1. THE ORDER OF CANADA

C.C. O.C. C.M.

Terms:

The Order of Canada was established as the centerpiece of Canada's system of honours to pay tribute to those who exemplify the highest qualities of citizenship and whose contributions enrich the lives of their contemporaries. Only Canadian citizens are eligible to be members but honorary members can be non-Canadians who have served Canada. The Queen of Canada is the Sovereign Head of the Order and the Governor  General is the Chancellor and Principal Companion. The Order has three levels: Companion, Officer, and Member.

COMPANION:

— For outstanding achievement and merit of the highest degree, especially service to Canada or to humanity at large. A maximum of 15 may be appointed in any one year with a maximum of 150 Companions.

OFFICER:

— For achievement and merit of a high degree, especially service to Canada or to humanity at large. A maximum of 46 Officers may be appointed per year. (increased from 40 to 46 in 1983)

MEMBER:

— For distinguished service in or to a particular locality, group, or field of activity. A maximum of 92 Members may be appointed annually.
— Half of the annual quotas are appointed on 1 July and half are appointed on 1 January. (Members quota increased from 80 to 92 in 1983)

Obverse:

A Maple Leaf with an annulus which bears the motto DESIDERANTES MELIOREM PATRIAM (They desire a better country) and surmounted by a St. Edward's Crown.

Reverse:

CANADA within a circle and a serial number in a box below.

Description:

A six pointed snow flake. All levels have the annulus in red.

Companion:

$2^1/_4$" across; enamelled white and edged in gold; maple leaf is red.

Officer:

$1^7/_8$" across; enamelled white and edged in gold; maple leaf is gold.

Member:

$1^1/_2$" across; enamelled white and edged in silver; maple leaf is silver.

Mounting:
Companion and Officer have a small link with a small ring attached. A larger ring is attached to the small ring and the ribbon passes through this for wearing around the neck. The Members badge has a small link with a large ring attached through which the ribbon passes for wearing on the left breast. All three badges are worn by women recipients on the left side and are suspended from a bow.

Ribbon:
1 1/2" inches; Red with a broad White centre (3/4"); a maple leaf of red, gold, or silver is worn on the ribbon in undress. Neck badge ribbon is full-size during the day and miniature in evening dress (black or white tie).

Dates:
Instituted 17 April 1967 with the first members appointed 1 July 1967. The Order was amended in 1972 to expand it from the two level of Companions and Medal of Service to the current three levels. All recipients of the Medal of Service were made Officers of the Order.

Issued:

Total Issued:	TOTALS	COMPANIONS	OFFICERS	MEMBERS
Appointed:	2,099	242*	832	1,025**
Living:	1,601	145	614	842**
Elevations:	42	—	30	12

January 1985 (* includes 8 ex-officio, ** one honourary to Zena Sheardowne)

Examples:
Governors General Roland Michener, Jules Leger, Edward Schreyer, Jean Sauve

Military:
General J.A. Dextraze, C.C., C.B.E., C.M.M., D.S.O., C.D.
General J.V. Allard, C.C., C.B.E., D.S.O., E.D., C.D.
Lt. Gen. E.L.M. Burns, C.C., D.S.O., O.B.E., M.C., C.D.
Lt. Gen. H.D. Graham, O.C., C.V.O., C.B.E., D.S.O., E.D., C.D.
Maj. Gen. G.R. Pearkes, V.C., P.C., C.C., C.B., D.S.O., M.C., C.D.

Sports:
Jean Beliveau, Phil Esposito, Nancy Greene, Gordie Howe, Bobby Hull, Russ Jackson, Ferguson Jenkins, Harry Jerome, Guy Lafleur, Bobby Orr, Karen Magnussen, Maurice Richard, Elaine Tanner, Ron Turcotte, Wayne Gretzsky, Alex Baumann, Gaetan Boucher.

Entertainment:
Pierre Berton, Roger Doucet, Maureen Forrester, Lorne Greene, Rene Lecavalier, Christopher Plummer, Gordon Sinclair, Jehane Benoit.

Politicians:
Iona Campognolo, Lionel Chevrier, Jean Drapeau, Stephen Juba, Earnest Manning, Douglas Harkness, OC, GM, ED.

Law:
J.V. Clyne, Emmett Hall, Walter Owen, J. Wilson.

2. THE ORDER OF MILITARY MERIT

Terms:

C.M.M. O.M.M. M.M.M.

The Order of Military Merit was established to provide a worthy means of recognizing conspicuous merit and exceptional service by members of the Canadian Forces (CF), both Regular and Reserve Forces. The Queen of Canada is the Sovereign of the Order and the Governor General is Chancellor of the Order and a Commander of the Order. The Chief of the Defence Staff is, by virtue of that office, Principal Commander of the Order.

The Order comprises three degrees:

Commander — This degree makes up 6% of the total membership;
Officer — This degree makes up 30% of the total membership;
Member — This degree makes up 64% of the total membership.

In any year, the Governor General may appoint a number of eligible persons to the Order that does not exceed one-tenth of one percent (0.1%) of the average number of persons who were members of the CF during the immediately preceding year. This currently works out to about 100 members annually. There is no overall maximum membership in any degree. Only members of the CF are eligible to be appointed to the Order as full members but servicemen of the armed forces of a country other than Canada are eligible to be made honorary member of the Order.

COMMANDER
— Appointments are made for outstanding meritorious service in duties of great responsibility.

OFFICER
— Appointments are made for outstanding meritorious service in duties of responsibility.

MEMBER
— Appointments are made for exceptional service or performance of duty. Members and Officers may be appointed to the next higher degree but no member shall hold more than one appointment at any time.

Obverse:
A Maple Leaf within an anulus which bears the words • MERIT • MERITE • CANADA. The annulus is surmounted by a St. Edward's Crown.

Reverse:
Plain; serial numbers were stamped into the edge of the lower arm until 1983 when the serial number was stamped on the reverse.

Description:

The badge of the Order is a blue enamelled straight-end cross pattee (four arms narrow at the centre and expanding towards the ends). The badge of the Commander and Officer is edged in gold and that of the Member is edged in silver. The Commander has a red Maple Leaf in the centre; the Officer has a gold Maple Leaf, and; the Member has a silver Maple Leaf. The annulus is red with gold letters (silver for Members).

Mounting:

The Commander's badge has a small link with a small ring attached. A larger ring is attached to the small ring and the ribbon passes through this for wearing around the neck. The Officer's and Member's badge has a small ring at the top through which another small ring attaches to a ring at the bottom of a laurelled bar (3 rings). The bar is gold for Officers and silver for Members. The Officer's and Member's wear their badges on the left breast. Women may wear their badges from a bow.

Ribbon:

1 1/2" inches wide; Blue with Gold edges (3/16"); Until 1983, a maple leaf of red, gold or silver was worn on the ribbon in undress uniform. After 1983, the lapel badge (blue cross with maple leaf in the centre) is worn on the ribbon in undress with the maple leaf being red, gold or silver to signify the level. Promotions within the Order are indicated by wearing the lapel badges of current and previous levels on a single ribbon.

Dates:

Instituted in July 1972 (General Sharp first member, 1 July 1972).

Issued:

Issued:	TOTALS	COMMANDERS	OFFICERS	MEMBERS
Appointed:	1388*	82	358	948
Elevations:	9	—	4	5

January 1985 * includes 4 Govenor Generals

Examples:

General J. Dextraze, CC, CBE, CMM, DSO, CD
Colonel A. Matheson, OMM, CM, CD
Adjuc Philippe Latulippe, CM, MMM, CD
MWO Donald George LeMoine, MMM, MM, CD
Captain Keith Trevor Gathercole, S.C., O.M.M., C.D.
MCpl Roderick Campbell, M.B., M.M.M., C.D.
Capt. (N) D.J. Kidd, D.S.C., O.M.M., C.D., M.D.
Lt. General William Carr, C.M.M., D.F.C., C.D.

3. CROSS OF VALOUR

Terms:

All Canadian citizens, both civilians and members of the Canadian Forces, are eligible for this award. Persons who are not Canadian citizens may receive this award if they perform an act of bravery in Canada, or perform a comparable act of bravery outside Canada that merits recognition by Canada as an act in the interest of Canada. The  Cross of Valour is awarded only for ACTS OF CONSPICUOUS COURAGE IN CIRCUMSTANCES OF EXTREME PERIL. (also awarded posthumously)

Bar:

A gold maple leaf is worn on the larger ring for a 2nd act of bravery.

Obverse:

A gold cross of four equal limbs, enamelled red and edged in gold with superimposed in the centre, a gold maple leaf surrounded by a gold wreath of laurel.

Reverse:

The Royal Cypher and crown in the upper arm; VALOUR VAILLANCE below the cypher along the two lateral arms: recipients name and date of the incident below.

Description:

A gold cross enamelled red of four equal limbs, 2 inches across.

Mounting:

A link with a small ring through which a large broad ring attaches. The Cross is worn around the neck or in a bow for ladies.

Ribbon:

1 1/2 inches; Light Crimson (Red). A miniature cross is worn on the ribbon in undress. (subsequent awards would add a second cross).

Dates:

1972 (one of three awards replacing Order of Canada-Medal of Courage)

Issued:

14 to March 1985

Examples

Mr. Kenneth Bishop, CV; Miss Mary Dohey, CV, RN; Mr. Lester Fudge CV; Corporal Amedeo Garrammone, CV; Mr. Thomas Hynes, CV; Major Rene Marc Jalbert, CV, CD (awarded July 1984); Mrs. Anna Lang, CV; M. Gaston Langelier, CV; Mr. Harold Miller, CV; CWO Vaino Partanen, CV, CD; Mr. Martin Sceviour, CV; Sgt. Lewis John Stringer, CV, CD; Mrs. Jean Swedberg, CV; Corporal Robert G. Teather, CV, (RCMP).

4. STAR OF COURAGE

S.C. or E.C.

Terms:
All Canadian citizens (and foreign persons as described for the Cross of Valour) are eligible for the award of the Star of Courage. The Star of Courage is awarded only for ACTS OF CONSPICUOUS COURAGE IN CIRCUMSTANCES OF GREAT PERIL.

Bar:
A gold bar with a gold maple leaf in the centre is awarded for subsequent acts of courage.

Obverse:
In the centre, a gold maple leaf surrounded by a gold laurel wreath.

Reverse:
In the upper arm, a crown; below that E II R (royal cypher); below that the word COURAGE. The recipient's name and date of incident below Courage.

Description:
A silver star of four points with a maple leaf in each of the angles. The star is 1 ½ inches across. Maple Leaf in gold is surrounded by a gold wreath of laurel in the centre.

Mounting:
A small ball on the top point has a large ring attached through which the ribbon passes. Worn on left breast or from a bow by women.

Ribbon:
1 ¼ inches wide; Light Crimson (Red) with two Blue stripes (³/₁₆" wide and ⅛" from each edge). Gold maple leaf worn if bar awarded.

Dates:
1972 Current.

Issued:
248 (54 posthumous; 5 recipients have died, no bars, to 4 May 1985).

Examples:
Mr. Bob Grant, S.C. and Mr. Brian Clegg, S.C., were awarded the Star in September 1980 for rescuing a nurse from Devil Gap 28 March 1979. Clegg flew the helicopter in a snow storm and Grant pulled the nurse from the icy water while sitting on the helicopter's skids.

Corporal Craig Douglas Seager, SC, MB, CD was awarded the SC on 26/07/82 as a member of 442 Search & Rescue Unit at CFB Comox. He was awarded the MB on 21/07/84 and thus became the first Canadian to win two different Canadian Bravery Decorations.

5. MEDAL OF BRAVERY

Terms:
All Canadian citizens, both civilians and members of the Canadian Forces, are eligible for the award of the Medal of Bravery. Persons who are not Canadian citizens may receive the award as described for the Cross of Valour. The Medal of Bravery is awarded only for acts of bravery in hazardous circumstances. It may be awarded posthumously.

Obverse:
Maple Leaf surrounded by a wreath of laurel.

Reverse:
Royal Cypher in the centre with a crown above it. Around the edge on the left is the word BRAVERY and on the right BRAVOURE with a small flower separating the two words at the base.

Description:
The medal is circular, silver, 1.42 inches across.

Mounting:
Fleur de lis attached to top of medal and to bottom of a straight bar. Medal is worn on the left breast or in a bow for women.

Bar:
A silver bar with a silver maple leaf in the centre is awarded for subsequent acts of bravery.

Ribbon:
Light Crimson (Red) with three Blue stripes ($^1/_8$"), one in the middle and the other two $^1/_8$" from the ribbon edge. Ribbon is $1^1/_4$ inches wide. A silver maple leaf is worn on the ribbon in undress if a bar is awarded.

Dates:
July 1, 1972

Issued:
646 (3 posthumous; 4 recipients have died, first bars awarded to Lt. Marcel Mailloux and Corporal Patrick McBride, to 4 May 1985).

Examples:
Corporal Sylvain Ross, MB and Corporal Robin Taylor, MB, aircraft technicians on HMCS Iroquois, displayed considerable daring and professionalism in readying the flight deck for the rescue of eleven seamen from the disabled No. 5 Ho Ming, floundering off the coast of Newfoundland on 4-5 December 1983.

6. ORDER OF CANADA — MEDAL OF COURAGE   C.M.

Terms:

When the Order of Canada was introduced in 1967, a Medal of
Courage was to be awarded to any
person who performs an act of conspicuous courage in circumstances
of great danger. The medal was
never awarded and was superceded
by the Cross of Valour, Star of
Courage and Medal of Bravery.

Obverse:

A six pointed snow flake with a
single Maple Leaf in a circle in the
centre and surmounted by a St. Edward's Crown.

Reverse:

An annulus bearing the word COURAGE.

Description:

Six pointed snow flake, 1.3 inches across, gold in colour.

Mounting:

A ball with a large ring through which the ribbon passes for wearing on the
left breast. Women would have worn the medal from a bow.

Ribbon:

1 1/4 inches wide; Red with a White centre (^{10}/$_{16}$" wide). - Gold Maple Leaf.

Dates:

1967 to 1972 when superceded by the three Canadian Bravery awards.

Issued:

Nil — it was realized that one award could not cover the wide range of brave
deeds and thus the Medal of Courage was not awarded.

Note:

In the original membership of the Order of Canada (1967), had the Medal of
Courage been awarded, the recipient would have been a member of the
Order of Canada. With the change in 1972, recipients of the Canadian Bravery awards are not members of the Order of Canada. Thus in the original
terms of the Order of Canada, people appointed Companions, people
awarded the Medal of Service and people awarded the Medal of Courage
would all be "Members" of the Order of Canada.

7. THE ORDER OF CANADA — MEDAL OF SERVICE S.M.

Terms:
When the Order of Canada was introduced in 1967, its members were either Companions of recipients of the Medal of Sevice. The Medal of Service was awarded for achievement and merit of high degree, especially service to Canada or humanity at large. A maximum of 50 could be awarded annually. The medal was replaced by the degree of Officer of the Order of Canada in 1972 and all recipients of the medal could exchange their medals for the badge of Officer.

Obverse:
A six pointed snow flake with a single Maple Leaf in a circle in the centre and surmounted by a St. Edward's Crown.

Reverse:
An annulus bearing the word S E R V I C E. Naming was in 2 lines on the lower arm: initials on the first line for males, Christian names on the first line for females, and surnames on the second line.

Description:
Six pointed snow flake, 1 1/2 inches from point to point, silver in colour

Mounting:
A ball on the top point to which is attached a large ring. The medal was worn on the left breast from a straight ribbon by men and from a bow by ladies.

Ribbon:
1 1/4 inches; Red with a broad White centre ($^{10}/_{16}$" wide). Silver Maple Leaf

Dates:
1 July 1967 to 1 May 1972 (superceded by Officer of the Order of Canada).

Issued:
268 — 196 were exchanged for Officer's badges. Of the 196, 189 were melted down by the Mint making the medal very rare.

Example:
Mr. Russell Stanley Jackson: awarded S.M. 19 December 1969 and converted to O.C. 1 July 1972. A football player with the Ottawa Rough Riders, he won 3 Schenley Awards as the Most Outstanding Player in the C.F.L. and 4 Schenleys as the Most Outstanding Canadian Player. A math teacher and Principal in the Ottawa & Toronto School Systems.

8. CANADA MEDAL 1943

Terms:
The Medal was to have been awarded for the recognition of meritorious services by citizens of Canada, whether civilians or members of the Armed Forces who rendered valuable and meritorious service. Only 14 were struck and none were issued.

Obverse:
Crowned head of George VI, facing left with the legend around the edge GEORGIVS VI D. G: BR: OMN: REX ET INDIAE IMP:

Reverse:
Within a wreath of maple leaves, the Escutcheon of the Coat of Arms of Canada surmounted by a crown. CANADA on a ribbon scroll below.

Description:
Circular, silver medal, 1.42 inches across.

Mounting:
Two ornamental arms (as per George VI CD) attach to a broad bar with the word MERIT (or MERITE) on it.

Ribbon:
Red-White-Red in equal widths; 1 1/4 inches wide.

Note:
14 were struck; 7 had MERIT and 7 had MERITE on the bar. All were stamped 'specimen' on the edge. A Mint prototype has found its way onto the market.

Terms:

The Order has one class and does not confer knighthood. It was introduced in 1902 as a very special distinction to those supreme in the fields of arts, literature and science and occasionally to military leaders in time of war. It is limited to 24 members who are citizens of a country of the British Commonwealth. It may also be awarded to foreigners as "Honorary Members".

Badge:

A gold cross, pattee convexed, enamelled red, edged blue, with, in the centre of the obverse, the words FOR MERIT on a blue ground. The cross is surmounted by a Tudor crown and worn round the neck. Military recipients wear a badge with crossed swords between the arms of the cross. Worn around neck.

Ribbon:

2 inches wide; Half Blue, half Crimson. (Garter and Bath)

Examples:

3 Canadians only: Dr. Wilder Penfield   01.01.53
            Rt. Hon. Mackenzie King   17.11.47
            Rt. Hon. Lester B. Pearson   28.05.71

10. THE ORDER OF THE COMPANIONS OF HONOUR C.H.

Terms:

The Order has one class and does not confer knighthood. It was introduced in June 1917 to honour those who have rendered conspicuous service of national importance. It is limited to the Sovereign and 65 members.

Badge:

An oval-shaped badge consisting of a gold medallion with an oak tree, hanging from one branch being a shield of the Royal Arms, and on the right a knight armed and in armour, mounted on a horse. The badge has a blue border with the motto IN ACTION FAITHFUL AND IN HONOUR CLEAR in gold letters and is surmounted by the Imperial Crown. Worn around the neck.

Ribbon:

1 1/2 inches, wide; Carmine with borders of gold thread.

Examples:

7 Canadians:

Rt. Honourable Vincent Massey, P.C., C.C., C.H., C.D.

Rt. Honourable John Diefenbacker, C.H.

General A. McNaughton, C.H., C.B., C.M.G., D.S.O., C.D. & three Bars

General H.D.G. Crerar, C.H., C.B., D.S.O.

Dr. Charles Best, C.H.

Mr. Arnold Smith, OC, C.H. (awarded OC December 1984)

Rt. Honourable P.E. Trudeau, P.C., C.H. (made a Companion 1984)

11. THE MOST HONOURABLE ORDER OF THE BATH
G.C.B.   K.C.B.   C.B.

Terms:
The Order has a civil and a military division and it is awarded for service of the highest order (in wartime it is awarded to Senior Officers who must have been mentioned in despatches). It is a three class order: (I) Knights Grand Cross (maximum 22 military and 12 civil); (II) Knight Commander, and (III) Companion. The first two grades confer Knighthood and the right to bear the title "Sir". Canadians cannot receive knighthoods after 22 May 1919 (except for a brief period around 1933).

Badge: *MILITARY:* A gold Maltese cross of eight points, enamelled white, each point tipped with a gold ball, and in each angle between the arms of the cross a gold lion. The central device consists of the rose, thistle and shamrock issuing from a sceptre and three crowns. Surrounding the central device is a red enamel circle with the motto TRIA JUNCTA IN UNO in gold. Around this circle are two branches of laurel, enamelled green, and below is a blue enamel scroll with ICH DIEN in gold. *CIVIL:* An oval badge with the motto and in the centre, the rose, thistle and shamrock issuing from a sceptre and the three crowns.

Totals:
G.C.B.—2 military & 2 civil; K.C.B.—20 Military & 5 Civil
C.B.—125 military & 25 civil.

Examples:
LGen. Sir A.W. Currie, KCB, KCMG
AVM McEwen, C.B., M.C. DFC.
AM R. Leckie, CB, DSO, DSC, DFC;
LGen. Guy Simmonds, CB, CBE, DSO.
Brigadier J.M. Rockingham, CB, CBE, DSO, ED.

12. THE MOST DISTINGUISHED ORDER OF ST. MICHAEL AND ST. GEORGE G.C.M.G. K.C.M.G. C.M.G.

Terms:

Established in 1818 and awarded to citizens of the Commonwealth who have rendered distinguished services in the former colonies and in foreign affairs. It is a three class Order: (I) Knights Grand Cross (G.C.M.G.); (II) Knights Commander (K.C.M.G.), and; (III) Companions (C.M.G.). The first two classes confer Knighthood so cannot be given to Canadians after 1919 (and briefly around 1933).

Badge:

Gold seven-pointed star (v-shaped extremities), enamelled white and edged gold and surmounted by the Imperial Crown. In the centre on the obverse is a representation in enamel of St. Michael encountering Satan and on the reverse, St. George on horseback fighting the dragon. These representations are surounded by a circle of blue enamel, with the motto: AUSPICIUM MELIORIS AEVI (Token of a better age). The first two classes also have a Star.

Ribbon:
1 1/2 inches; equal stripes of Blue-Red-Blue.

Totals:
G.C.M.G.—25   K.C.M.G.—125   C.M.G.—300

Examples:
G.C.M.G.—Wilfred Laurier; R.J. Cartwright; Oliver Mowat.
K.C.M.G.—LGen. A.W. Currie KCB, KCMG; Dr. J.A. Grant; S. Fleming.
C.M.G.—MGen. W.W. Foster CMG, DSO,VD.

13. THE ROYAL VICTORIAN ORDER AND MEDAL
G.C.V.O.   K.C.V.O.   C.V.O.   L.V.O.   M.V.O.   R.V.M.

Terms:

The Order was established in 1896 and is conferred for extraordinary import or personal services to the Sovereign or to the Royal Family. This Order (like the Order of Merit) is the Sovereign's personal perogative (i.e. not made on the advice of a Minister or government). Since the Queen is the Sovereign Head of Canada, it can and is awarded to Canadians by the Queen. The Order has five grades: (I) Knights (Dames) Grand Cross; (II) Knights (Dames) Commanders, (there two levels confer knighthood and are therefore not awarded to Canadians any longer); (III) Commanders (CVO); (IV) Lieutenant of the Royal Victorian Order (LVO) — changed on 31 December 1984 to LVO from Member, fourth class; (V) Member (MVO) — changed to just Member from Member, fifth class on 31 December 1984. The Medal was also upgraded in 1984 and while its award still does not make one a member of the Royal Victorian Order, those awarded the medal may now use the post-nominal letters RVM.

Badge:

A white-enamelled Maltese Cross in the centre of which is an oval of crimson enamel with the cypher VRI (superimposed one letter on the other) in gold. Encircling the cypher is a blue enamel riband with the name VIC-TORIA in gold letters around the bottom. An Imperial Crown sits atop the riband. A CVO wears a 2 inch badge around the neck; an LVO wears a 1½ inch badge on the left breast from a straight ribbon (enamelled white badge) and an MVO wears an unenamelled silver cross in the same manner (ladies may wear their badge from a bow). The medals bear the uncrowned effigy of the reigning Sovereign. The medal is smaller than most being only 1.1 inches across and is issued in gold, silver (most commonly) and bronze.

Ribbon:

1¼ inches; Blue with red-white-red narrow edges; (CVO ribbon is 1¾" wide).

Totals:
G.C.V.O. — 5, K.C.V.O. — 5, C.V.O. — 33, L.V.O./M.V.O. — 35, R.V.M. — 4, since 1977

Examples:
Maj. J.H. Leduc MVO 1973; Maj. C.G.G. Bristowe, MVO 1973; LCol J.G.C. Bernier, LVO 1976; Maj. D.C. Summers, LVO 1978; Maj. R.G. Simard, LVO 1978; Michael Pitfield CVO 1982; Laurence J. Wallace, OC, CVO 1983;

Silver RVMs:
Miss H. Donner, RVM (19 Oct. 1977)
Mr. J. Nadon, RVM (19 Oct. 1977)
Constable A.L.J. Giradin, RVM (6 Aug. 1978); RCMP
Mr. A.H. Johnson, RVM (28 Dec. 1979).

14. THE ROYAL VICTORIAN CHAIN

Terms:
Often considered the highest grade of the Royal Victorian Order, it has no connection with this Order. It was established in 1902 and is conferred as a special mark of the Sovereign's favour and is given rarely.

Badge:

The chain is of gold and consists of three Tudor roses, two shamrocks and two lotus flowers, connected by a slender double trace of gold chain. At the bottom of the front loop is a centrepiece consisting of the Royal Cypher in enamel surrounded by a wreath and surmounted by a crown. From this centre piece hangs a jewelled replica of the Badge of the Royal Victorian Order. All Chains are numbered and must be returned to the Central Chancery upon the death of the recipient. There is no ribbon with this award and there are no postnominal initials used to indicate this award.

Examples:

Only two Canadian reipients:

Rt. Hon. Vincent Massey, CC, CH, CD — 22 July, 1960

Rt. Hon. Roland Michener, CC, CMM, CD. — 3 August 1973; Mr. Michener's Chain is No. 52, previously worn by the Rt. Hon. Lawrence Roger (Earl of Scarborough) KG, GCSI, GCIE, GCVO, TD, who died 29 June 1969.

15.   IMPERIAL SERVICE ORDER   I.S.O.

Terms:

The Order was established in 1902 to recognized meritorious service by active members of the Civil Service throughout the Commonwealth. It has one class only, Companion, and the recipient must have at least 25 years service or 16 years in unhealthy places abroad. It is limited to 700 Companions.

Badge:

It is a seven pointed star of silver with a gold medallion in the centre which bears the Royal Cypher. Around the Cypher is a circle with the words FOR FAITHFUL SERVICE. The words and cypher are in blue enamel and a Crown surmounts the ring. It is worn from the left breast. The badge for a woman has a silver laurel wreath replacing the star and is worn from a bow.

Ribbon:

1 1/2 inches; Crimson-Blue-Crimson in equal stripes.

Totals:

91 to Canadians (GRI — 33   GVR — 14   Ed VII — 44)

Example:

LCol. A.L. Jarvis, I.S.O., V.D. was awarded the ISO (Ed VII) for service as a senior civil servant and the VD (Ed VII) as LCol. Commanding the G.G.F.G. He was also awarded the Canadian General Service Medal (bar Fenian Raid 1870) as a very young bugler with the Ottawa Garrison Artillery, and the Colonial Auxiliary Forces Long Service Medal (Victoria issue) for his time in the ranks.

16. IMPERIAL SERVICE MEDAL

Terms:
Awarded in a like manner to the Imperial Service Order but unlimited in number and awarded to all branches of the civil service.

Bar:
No bars

Obverse:
a) Edward VII and early George V were a star similar to the Order but in bronze rather than silver.
b) George V uncrowned bust — GEORGIVS V · D.G. BRITT OMN : RED F.D. IND : IMP :
c) George V crowned bust — GEORGIVS V · D.G. BRITT · OMN : REX · ET · INDIAE · IMP ·
d) George VI crowned bust — GEORGIVS VID G : BR : OMN : REX ET INDAE IMP.
e) Elizabeth II crowned bust — ELIZABETH II D : G : BR : OMN : REGINA F : D

Reverse:
A nude male seated with trees and a wall in the background with the words "FOR FAITHFUL SERVICE" at the bottom

Description:
Circular, 1¼ inches, silver.

Mounting:
Ring suspender with single toe claw.

Ribbon:
1½ inches Crimson-Blue-Crimson in equal stripes (watered)

Dates:
Authorized 8 August 1902

Issued:
7,121 to Canadian (no Elizabeth II known to be issued)

17. THE MOST EXCELLENT ORDER OF THE BRITISH EMPIRE

G.B.E. K.B.E.
C.B.E. O.B.E.
M.B.E. (B.E.M.)

Terms:

The *CIVIL DIVISION* is awarded by the British Government for services to the Empire (Commonwealth) at home, in India and in the Dominions and Colonies. The *MILITARY DIVISION* is awarded for services in the field or before the enemy or for services to the Empire (Commonwealth).

The Order has five classes plus the British Empire Medal:

1. **Knights (Dames) Grand Cross (G.B.E.):** — wear a star on the left breast and the badge on the left hip from a ribbon (95 mm. wide) passing over the right shoulder. 5 G.B.E.s to Canadians.
2. **Knights (Dames) Commander (K.B.E.):** — wear a star on the left breast and the badge suspended round the neck from a ribbon (44 mm. wide). 41 K.B.E.s to Canadians.
3. **Commander (C.B.E.):** — wear the badge suspended round the neck from a ribbon (44 mm. wide). 310 C.B.E.s to Canadians.
4. **Officers (O.B.E.):** — wear a silver-gilt badge on the left breast from a ribbon (38 mm. wide). Women wear the badge from a bow. 1200 approximately awarded to Canadians.
5. **Members (M.B.E.):** — wear a silver badge as per the O.B.E. Over 2100 awarded to Canadians.
6. **British Empire Medal (B.E.M.):** — described separately.

Bar:

A silver emblem of two oak leaves is worn on the riband when the appointment to the Order is for Gallantry.

Obverse:

Until 1936, the badge contained a representation of Britannia with the motto FOR GOD AND THE EMPIRE in a circle around her. The post 1936 (current) badge contains the conjoint bust of King George V and Queen Mary facing left with the motto FOR GOD AND THE EMPIRE in a circle around them.

Reverse:

A rope circle with the Royal Cypher surmounted by a crown. Hallmarks on the lower limb.

Description:

The badge is a cross patonce (four arms with three points at each end of a broad arm), with a crown on the top arm. The first three classes are of silver-gilt, with the arms enamelled pearl-grey; the OBE is of silver gilt; and the MBE is made of silver. The neck badges are 2$^1/_2$" across and the breast badges (OBE, MBE) are 2 inches across.

Mounting:

Ring attached to the top of the Crown through which the ribbon passes.

Ribbon:

Pre -1936, Civil — Purple (1$^1/_2$ inches wide in undress).

Pre -1936, Military — Purple, with a narrow central Scarlet stripe.

Post-1936, Civil — Rose-Pink with Pearl-Grey edges. (1$^1/_2$" wide).

Post 1936, Military — Rose-Pink with Pearl-Grey edges and a central narrow Pearl-Grey stripe.

Dates:

Founded in June 1917: After 22 May, 1919, Canadians were not eligible to receive awards which granted titular honour (G.B.E. & K.B.E.) This policy was reversed in 1933 and Canadians were included in three honour lists. Parliament again instituted the no titular honour ban and this has remained in effect ever since. Canadians were included on British Honour Lists from 24 July 1942 until 1 July 1946 for non-titular honours such as the C.B.E., O.B.E. & M.B.E. as a special concession during WWII. On 1 July 1946, civilians were no longer eligible for war honours but those for the military continued. This award has been largely replaced by the Order of Canada and Order of Military Merit but Canadian military personnel still receive the award on accasion. Major J.G. Easson was awarded the M.B.E. 1 August 1980. He is a member of the 8th Canadian Hussars.

Issued:

over 3700 all 5 classes (specific numbers listed above).

Examples:

General Sir Neil Ritchie, G.B.E., K.C.B., D.S.O., M.C.
Air Marshall W.A. Curtis, C.B., C.B.E., D.S.C., E.D.
Air Marshall C.R. Slemon, C.B., C.B.E., C.D.
BGen E.A.C. Amy, D.S.O., O.B.E., M.C., C.D.
Hon. Henry P. Bell-Irving, D.S.O., O.B.E., E.D., C.D.
Col. Gordon Reay, M.B.E., C.D. — awarded 1978
Major J.G. Easson, M.B.E., C.D. — awarded 1980
Mr. C.A. Axworthy, O.B.E. (civil) 1981
Mr. B.W. Ashton, M.B.E. (civil) 1982

18.   ORDER OF ST. JOHN   K.St.J   C.St.J.   O.St.J.   S.B.St.J.

(The Most Venerable Order of the Hospital of St. John of Jerusalem)

Terms:

Persons are admitted to the Order in any grade under the following terms: (a) professes the Christian Faith; (b) is a citizen or national of a country which is a member of the Commonwealth or of Eire, South Africa, Tonga, or Pakistan; (c) has performed or is prepared to perform good service for the Order; and (d) has undertaken to conform to all the Rules of the Order. A person who does not fit (a) or (b) may be made an Associate Member.

The Sovereign Head of the Order is Queen Elizabeth II and the Grand Prior is H.R.H. The Duke of Gloucester. The Governor General of Canada is the Prior for Canada. The Order follows the five-Grade Orders of Chivalry; (I) Bailiff and Dame Grand Cross; (II) Knight and Dame of Justice and of Grace; (III) Commander, Brother and Sister; (IV) Officer, Brother and Sister and; (V) Serving Brother and Serving Sister. The maximum number of Bailiff Grand Cross is 12 at any one time and Canada has one, BGen. Cyrille J. Laurin, OBE. The maximum number of Dame Grand Cross is 7 at any one time and Canada has one, Mlle Yvette Loiselle. The letters shown at the top are used only for official correspondence within the Order and are not authorized for use otherwise.

Badge:

The badge consists of a true Maltese cross, an eight-pointed cross in white enamel set in base metal (silver until 1951). The cross is embellished in each of its principal angles with a lion and a unicorn (the lion being in the top left and bottom right angles).

Ribbon:

Black watered. A small silver cross is worn on the ribbon in undress. A lady wears her badge as a bow on the left breast. The ribbon size for men of the three lowest grades is 1 1/2 inches and for women 1 1/4 inches. The ribbon size for a Knight is 2 inches and for a Dame 1 1/4 inches. Bailiff Grand Cross wears the badge from a 4 inches wide ribbon; Dame G.C. from a 2 1/4 inch ribbon.

Total Issued:

The total number of Canadians currently holding the grade is given.

BAILIFF (DAME) GRAND CROSS: (G.C.St.J)

The Star is in white enamel set in gold, 3 5/8 inches across and worn on the left breast. It is not embellished (no lions or unicorns). The badge is 3 1/4 inches across, embellished and suspended from the ribbon by a ring. It is worn over the right shoulder from a 4 inch wide ribbon for Bailiffs, 2 1/4" for Dames.

KNIGHT (DAME) of JUSTICE and of GRACE: (K.St.J. — D.St.J.)

A person is made a Knight or Dame of Grace. To be re-classified as a Knight (Dame) of Justice, he or she must be able to satisfy the Genealogist of the Grand Priory that he or she is (a) entitled to bear arms, or (b) is the Prior of Priory. In Canada, persons are appointed Knights or Dames of Grace. Both sexes wear the star in white enamel (formerly set in silver and now in base metal), 3 inches across and embellished on the left breast. The badge is 2 1/4" across for Knights, suspended from the ribbon by a ring and worn round the neck from a ribbon 2" wide. The badge is 1 3/4 inches across and embellished for a Dame and is worn from a 1 1/4" wide ribbon as a bow on the left breast.

Total: 197 living Canadians plus approximately 10 per year (Jan. 1984)

Examples:

Hon. Henry Bell-Irving, OC, DSO, OBE, ED, CD.

Mr. Leo Stadnyk, 57 St. John Ambulance Division, New Westminster.

COMMANDER (BROTHER AND SISTER): (C.St.J.)

The badge of base metal and white enamel is 2 1/4" across for Brothers and 1 3/4" across for Sisters and embellished. It is worn round the neck from a 1 1/4" ribbon by Brothers and as a bow on the left breast by Sisters (ribbon 1 1/4" wide).

Total: 353 living Canadians plus approximately 25 per year (Jan. 1984)

Examples:

Mr. Wilf Shaw, 57 Division

Mr. Ed Liske, 57 New Westminister Division

OFFICER (BROTHER AND SISTER): (O.St.J.)

The badge is 1 3/4" across (1 1/4" for Sisters), white enamel set in base metal, embellished and worn on the left breast (bow for sisters). Ribbon: 1 1/2" & 1 1/4".

Total: 1,182 living Canadians plus approximately 90 per year (Jan. 1984)

Examples:

F.J. Blatherwick, 57 New Westminister Division

Surg. Cmdr. D.A. MacIver, CMM, CD, MB.

SERVING BROTHER AND SERVING SISTER: (S.B.St.J. — S.S.St.J.)

The old badge was circular, 1 1/2" across, metal rim, with the cross in white enamel (embellished) on a black enamel background. It is suspended from its ribbon by a ring, worn on the left breast from ribbon of 1 1/2" or 1 1/4" if a bow. In October 1980, the new badge was introduced. It is a simple St. John Cross, (embellished), 1 1/2" across, in a flat matte finish silver (looks grey), slightly humped, given a convex shape on the front face, with the embellishments in silver. It is worn suspended from the ribbon by a ring on the left breast from ribbon of 1 1/2" for Brothers and 1 1/4" for Sister (bow for Sisters).

In the Fall of 1984, the Serving Brother an Serving Sister crosses were rhodium plated and therefore appear bright silver.

Total: 2,932 living Canadians plus approximately 225 per year (Jan. 1984)

Deceased Bailiffs/Dames: Rt. Hon. Vincent Massey, Commissioner L.H. Nicholson OC, MBE (RCMP), Ms. Margaret MacLaren and Ms. E.K. Gilmour MBE.

19. VICTORIA CROSS

V.C.

Terms:
For most conspicuous bravery or some daring or pre-eminent act of valour or self-sacrifice or extreme devotion to duty in the presence of the enemy.

Bar:
For additional acts of bravery (none to Canadians; 3 in all).

Obverse:
A cross pattee with the Royal Crown surmounted by a lion guardant. Below the Crown, a scroll bearing the inscription: FOR VALOUR.

Reverse:
Raised edges with date of act engraved within a raised circle.

Description:
Cross, 1.5 inches, dull bronze

Mounting:
By a straight bar (ornamented with laurels), slotted for the ribbon with a V-lug below. A small link joins the V-lug to a semi-circular lug on the top of the cross.

Naming:
Rank, name, and regiment are engraved on the reverse of the mounting bar.

Ribbon:
1½ inches; Crimson (Dark Blue for Naval awards until 1918) with Miniature Cross

Dates:
29 January 1856 retroactive to 1854

Total Issued:
1,351 (3 bars) of which 93 were to Canadians and 13 Associated with Canada (Timothy O'Hea won the only V.C. in Canada) Canadian awards: 8 pre-WWI including 4 in South Africa; WWI-69; WWII-16 (only one WWI V.C. winner alive in 1985 — Charles Rutherford.

Examples:
WWII — John Osborne*, Charles Merritt, John Foote, Frederick Peters*, Paul Triquet*, Charles Hoey*, John Mahony, Andrew Mynarski*, David Hornell*, Ian Bazalgette*, David Currie, Ernie Smith, Aubrey Cosens*, Fred Tilston, Fred Topham*, Robert Hampton Gray*, VC, DSC.
* deceased

20. GEORGE CROSS G.C.

Terms:
Awarded for acts of the greatest heroism or of the most conspicuous courage in circumstances of extreme danger. The Cross is intended primarily for civilians and award in the military services is to be confined to actions for which purely military Honours are not normally granted and awarded for actions not in the face of the enemy.

Bar:
For additional acts of gallantry; none awarded to date.

Obverse:
St. George slaying a dragon within an annulus bearing the legend FOR GALLANTRY. The Royal Cypher GVI in each of the four corners of the cross with the VI inside a wide G.

Reverse:
Plain except for the naming.

Description:
Geneva Cross; 1.8 inches wide, silver.

Mounting:
Straight Laureled silver bar with the cross and the bar joined by a small silver ring which passes through the ring lugs of the medal and bar.

Naming:
Name, rank, Service, (Serial Number if not commissioned) and the date of the notification in the London Gazette.

Ribbon:
1 1/2 inches; Garter Blue; small cross always worn on ribbon as for the Victoria Cross. Women wear the medal from a bow.

Date:
May 1941 until replaced by the Canadian Bravery Awards.

Total Issued:
9 to Canadians

Examples:
Cpl. James Hendry, LAC Karl Gravell, LAC Ken Spooner, A/Sgt. John Rennie, F/O. Rod Gray all received the medal posthumously.
LAC Ernie Frost had his Empire Gallantry Medal converted to a G.C.
Mr. G.L. Bastien had his Albert Medal converted to a G.C.
A/C A.D. Ross, G.C., O.B.E., lost his right hand while rescueing a rear gunner from a burning aircraft. Lt. John M.S. Patton also received G.C.

21. DISTINGUISHED SERVICE ORDER D.S.O.

Terms:

Established for rewarding individual instances of meritorious or distinguished service in war. This is a purely military order and is only given to officers whose service has been marked by the special mention of his name in despatches for "distinguished services under fire, or under conditions equivalent to service in actual combat with the enemy.

Bars:

Awarded where the individual performs an approved act of gallantry which would have entitled him to the Order in the first place.

Obverse:

The badge consists of a gold cross, enamelled white, edged in gold, having in the centre within a wreath of laurel enamelled green, the Imperial Crown in gold.

Reverse:

Within a laurel wreath of enamelled green, the Royal Cypher in gold.

Description:

A gold cross, enamelled white, edged in gold.

Mounting:

A ring at the top of the medal attaches to a smaller ring at the bottom of a gold bar ornamented with laurel. A second gold bar ornamented with laurel is worn at the top of the ribbon.

Ribbon:

1⅛ inches wide; Red with Blue edges (ribbon is officially supposed to be 1" wide but available ribbon is 1⅛").

Dates:

Established in 1886

Issued:

Soudan - 1;   South Nigeria - 2;   South Africa - 20;
   World War I — 710 plus 89 first bars plus 15 second bars.
   World War II
             RCAF —   73 plus 6 first bars
              RAF —   16 plus 2 first bars (Cdns. in RAF)
              RCN —   8
            Army — 352 plus 15 first bars plus 3 second bars
     Korea - Army —   8 plus 1 second bar (Col. Stone, DSO, MC)
             RCN —   1 (Capt. J.V. Brock, DSO, DSC, CD)

22. ROYAL RED CROSS

Terms:

CLASS I: Awarded to a fully trained Nurse of the official Nursing Services who has performed an exceptional act of bravery and devotion to her post of duty. First class members are called Members. Class I is limited to 2 % of establishment.

CLASS II: Awarded as above except it includes Nurses and Nurses Aides and Volunteers. Class II membership is limited to 5 % of establishment and members are called Associates and use the initials A.R.R.C.

Bar:

For additional acts of gallantry (an A.R.R.C. would be raised to R.R.C.).
An R.R.C. receiving a second award would wear a bar.
An A.R.R.C. receiving a second award would be elevated to an R.R.C. and thus would not receive a bar.

Obverse:

CLASS I: Gold Cross patee, enameled red, edged in gold, having on the arms the words FAITH, HOPE, CHARITY, 1883 (top, left arm, right arm, bottom); in the centre is the head of the reigning Sovereign.
CLASS II: Cross as above but in frosted silver with a Maltese Cross enameled red superimposed and the head of the reigning Sovereign in the centre.

Reverse:

Class I: Reigning Monarch's Cypher and Crown in the centre.
Class II: Inscribed on the arms are the words, FAITH, HOPE, CHARITY & 1883, with the Reigning Monarch's Cypher and Crown in the centre.

Description:

Cross, 1³/₈ inches across, silver-gilt or silver enameled red.

Mounting:

Small ring at top of cross through which a larger ring passes. Badge is worn from a bow. When worn with other medals, an additional ring is added which is larger than the two existing rings and allows the ribbon to be attached through this third ring.

Ribbon:

1 inch; Light Blue centre ($^1/_2$") with Red edges ($^1/_4$").

Dates:

Instituted in April 1883 (First awarded to a Canadian in 1902)

Issued:

Class I - 129 plus 4 bars: Class II - 424

Examples:

Major M. Dewar, RRC — Matron in Chief RCAMC 1959-1962

Major E. Andrews, ARRC — M. in Chief RCAMC 1950-1959

Major D. Ballantine, ARRC M. in Chief RCAMC 1946-1950

Col. A. Neill, OBE, RRC. M. in Chief RCAMC 1945-1946

Cdr. M.G. Russel, RRC RCN Matron 1943-1947

LCdr. E. Ledingham, RRC RCN Matron 1947-1948

LCdr. F. Rutledge, RRC RCN Matron 1948-1954

SLdr. J. Porteous, ARRC RCAF Matron 1943-1945

Captain (Matron) E.B. Pense, RRC, CD (ARRC — WWII, RRC — Korea)

Lt. (N/S) J.I. Macdonald, ARRC, (for Korea)

Awards:

	Boer War	WWI	WWII	Korea
RRC	1	64	63	1
BARS	0	4	0	0
ARRC	0	253	170	1

Note:

In World War I, the awards were termed: Royal Red Cross (First Class) and Royal Red Cross (Second Class). The members of the Second Class were known as Associates an used the letters ARRC. In World War II, the First Class designation was dropped in favour of the term Royal Red Cross (RRC) and the term Second Class was dropped in favour of the term Associates of the Royal Red Cross (ARRC).

Note:

Georgina Fame Pope (1862-1938), First Matron of the Canadian Army Medical Corps. She served with distinction in the South Africa War and was the first Canadian to receive the Royal Red Cross for conspicuous service in the field

23. DISTINGUISHED SERVICE CROSS D.S.C.

Terms:
Awarded to Naval and Marine Officers, Commanders or below, including Warrant Officers (or equivalent), for meritorious or distinguished services before the enemy. Members of the Air Force and Army serving with the fleet were also eligible.

Bars:
For additional acts of gallantry. (Convex silver bar with a crown).

Obverse:
Royal Cypher surmounted by a Crown within a circle.

Reverse:
Plain, with year of the award engraved on the lower arm.

Description:
Plain silver cross pattee, convexed, $1^9/_{16}$ inches across.

Mounting:
Small ring at top through which a large ($^3/_4$") ring is attached.

Ribbon:
$1^3/_8$ inches; Navy Blue - White - Navy Blue in equal widths.

Dates:
Established June 1901 as Conspicuous Service Cross.
Changed to Distinguished Service Cross in October 1914.

Issued:
48 to Canadian Flyers WWI + 12 First Bars + 2 Second Bars
123 total in WWII plus 17 First Bars + 3 Second Bars
9 total in Korea plus 1 First Bar.

Examples:
Commander R.P. Welland, DSC & Bar, CD. (Bar Korea; HMCS Athabaskan
LCdr. J.H.G. Bovey, DSC HMCS Crusader
Captain (N) D.G. King, DSC, CD. HMCS Athabaskan
Lt. (N) Andrew Collier, CMM, DSC, CD.HMCS Cayuga
Cdr. Dunn Lantier, DSC, CD.HMCS Haida
Cdr. D.R. Saxon, DSC, CD.HMCS Cayuga
Cdr. R.M. Steele, DSC HMCS Nootka
Captain (N) P.D. Taylor, DSC, CD. HMCS Sioux
Lt. D.F. Tutte, DSC, CD HMCS Iroquois
Cdr. E.T.G. Madgwick, DSC, CD HMCS Huron
Above are the awards to RCN Officers for services in Korea.

Terms:

Awarded to Officers of the rank of Captain or lower including Warrant Officers, for gallant and distinguished services in action.

Bars:

For additional acts of bravery; straight silver bar with crown.

Obverse:

On each arm of the cross is an Imperial Crown and in the center of the cross is the Imperial and Royal Cypher of the reigning sovereign.

Reverse:

Plain, with year of the award engraved on lower arm.

Description:

Plain cross, 1³/₄ inches across, silver.

Mounting:

The ring at the top of the cross is joined to a ring at the bottom of the plain straight suspender by a small ring (3 rings).

Ribbon:

1³/₈ inches; watered White with central Purple stripe (¹/₂" wide).

Dates:

Established 28 December 1914.

Issued:

WWI — 2885 plus 294 bars plus 16 second bars
WWII — 678 plus 13 bars plus 1 second bar
Korea — 33 (8 George VI plus 25 EIIR)

Examples:

Lt. D.G. Loomis - 1st Battalion, Royal Canadian Regiment was awarded the M.C. when on 27 September 1952 he led a patrol against Hill 227 in Korea. Lt. Loomis and three of his men were wounded but they knocked out an enemy machine gun and its crew.

Lt. A.M. King - 1st Battalion, RCRs was awarded the M.C. when on 29 September 1952 when he led a rescue party to an outpost in Korea which had come under heavy fire. While effecting the rescue, he came under heavy fire but beat off the attack and brought the injured men to safety.

Canada Gazette, 28 March 1953, page 896

25. DISTINGUISHED FLYING CROSS D.F.C.

Terms:

Awarded to Officers and Warrant Officers for an act or acts of valour, courage or devotion to duty performed whilst flying in active operations against the enemy.

Bars:

For additional acts of bravery. Silver bar with an eagle in centre.

Obverse:

Cross flory terminated in the horizontal and base bars with bombs, the upper bar terminating with a rose, surmounted by another cross composed of aeroplane propellers charged in the centre with a roundel within a wreath of laurels, a rose winged ensigned by an Imperial Crown, theron the letters R A F.

Reverse:

Royal Cypher above the date 1918 in a circle; year of issue on lower arm.

Description:

Cross flory, 2 1/8 inches across, silver.

Mounting:

Ring at top of cross attached to the suspender by a small ring.

Ribbon:

1 1/4 inches; Violet and White alternate diagonal stripes 1/8" at 45° left to right. The Violet colour is to appear in the bottom left and upper right corners when viewed on the wearer's chest. Until 1919, the stripes were horizontal.

Dates:

Established 3 June 1918.

Issued:

WWI — 193 Crosses plus 9 first bars
WWII — 4018 Crosses plus 214 first bars plus 5 second bars
Korea — 2 (F/L Glover, RCAF & Capt. Tees, Canadian Army)

Examples:

Group Captain Gordon R. McGregor, OC, OBE, DFC, Croix de Guerre, Commander Order of Orange-Nassau, who became President of Air Canada, received the DFC for damaging or destroying eleven aircraft in the Battle of Britain. He, along with S/L McNab and F/O Dal Russell were the first members of the RCAF in WWII to be decorated.

Terms:
Awarded to Officers and Warrant Officers for an act or acts of valour, courage or devotion to duty whilst flying but not in active operations against an enemy.

Bar:
For Additional acts of bravery. (Same bar as to D.F.C.)

Obverse:
A thunderbolt in the form of a cross, the arms conjoined by wings, the base bar terminating with a bomb surmounted by another cross composed of aeroplane propellers, the four ends enscribed with letter G (top) R (left), V (bottom), I (right). Current Royal Cypher has E II R with the bottom blank. In the center is a roundel, theron, a representative of Hermes mounted on a hawk in flight bestowing a wreath. The whole is ensigned by an Imperial Crown.

Reverse:
Royal Cypher above date 1918 in a circle. Year of award appears on lower arm from 1939 on. Issued unnamed.

Description:
Silver cross, $1^5/8$ inches across. Full description above.

Mounting:
A small link at the top of the crown attaches to a slot in two sprigs of laurel. The laurel is attached to the bottom of a straight clasp.

Ribbon:
$1^1/4$ inches; Red and White alternate diagonal stripes $^1/8$" at 45° left to right. The Red colour is to appear in the bottom left and upper right corners when viewed on the wearer's chest. The stripes were originally horizontal (changed 1919).

Dates:
Established 3 June 1918.

Totals:

WW I — 71;	WWII — 431 (1 bar);	George VI after WWII — 11
Korea — 4	Post Korea (EIIR) — 11	

Examples:
F/L Daniel Michael Campbell, AFC, CD — awarded the last Air Force Cross presented to a Canadian for his actions of 18 July 1965 while in command of a Labrador helicopter. In closing darkness, he nestled his helicopter near the site of a plane crash and rescued all the survivors.

27. GEORGE MEDAL

Terms:
Awarded only for acts of great bravery and is intended primarily for civilians and awards to the military services is confined to actions for which purely military honours are not normally granted.

Bars:
For additional acts of bravery. (silver laurelled bar, slip on type)

Obverse:
1. George VI, crowned head, facing left. (two types of legends)
2. Elizabeth II, crowned head, facing right. (two types of legends)

Reverse:
St. George on horseback slaying the Dragon with the words THE GEORGE MEDAL around the top edge of the medal.

Description:
Circular, 1.42 inches, silver.

Mounting:
Ring suspender with single toe claw plus inward scroll claws.

Ribbon:
1¼ inches, Red with 5 equally spaced narrow Blue stripes.

Dates:
Established 24 September 1940 and extended to Canadians 15 May 1941.

Issued:
George VI RCAF - 21; Army - 13; RCN - 7 (plus 4 bars) Civilian - 1
E II R RCAF - 7; Army - 6; RCN - 6 RCMP - 2 Civilian - 9

Examples:

Lt. G.D. Cook, RCNVR	G.M. 29.07.41	Bar 10.02.42
T/Lt. D.J.P. O'Hagen, RCNVR	G.M. 27.06.41	Bar 9.06.42
T/LCDR. J.L. Harries, RCNVR	G.M. 28.09.43	Bar 15.05.45
Lt. G.H.O. Rundle, RCNR	G.M. 09.11.43	Bar 14.06.45

F/O E. Sabourin, G.M., C.D. — On 9 January 1957 at Rivers Manitoba, he was carrying out an air to ground rocket firing exercise in a T-33 jet aircraft armed with rockets with explosive heads instantaneous fused. Following his first attack, there was an explosion under the port wing. After gaining control of the aircraft at about 500 feet, he disregarded advice to abandon the T-33 and chose to land at Shilo which he did successfully. His actions saved a valuable aircraft and eliminated the possibility of the abandoned aircraft crashing into civilian or military accommodations in the area.

Terms:
Awarded to Warrant Officers, NCOs and men who have performed service of a distinctly gallant and distinguished nature in action in the field.

Bars:
For additional acts of gallantry. (Silver laurelled bar)

Obverse:
1. Edward VII, uncrowned, in Field Marshall's uniform, facing left.

2. George V, uncrowned, in Field Marshal's uniform, facing left.
3. George VI, crowned head, facing left. (two legends)
4. Elizabeth II, crowned head, facing right. (two legends)

Reverse:
The inscription in four lines: FOR / DISTINGUISHED / CONDUCT / IN THE FIELD with a horizontal line through a small oval wreath below the wording. One medal with the word CANADA above the 4 lines is known (an Edward VII medal).

Description:
Circular, 1.42 inches, silver.

Mounting:
Ornate scroll suspender with single toe claw and inward scroll claws.

Ribbon:
1 1/4 inches; Crimson with a Dark Blue (3/8") central stripe.

Dates:
Established for Canadians in 1902

Issued:
South Africa —   16 medals
  WWI — 1945 plus 36 first bars plus 1 second bar (Sgt. Sales)
  WWII — 163 plus 1 first bar (WO2 Rene Drapeau)
  Korea —   7 plus 1 first bar (Cpl. Major, R22eR)

Examples:
Pri. W.R. Mitchell, PPCLI Service in Korea.
Sgt. D.A. McCuish, PPCLI
L/Cpl. J.P.A. Harvey, R22eR
Cpl. E.W. Poole, RCAMC
Pri. R.E. Bauer, RCR
Sgt. R.G. Buxton, PPCLI (EIIR Medal)
Sgt. J.H. Richardson, PPCLI (EIIR Medal)

29. DISTINGUISHED SERVICE MEDAL   D.S.M.

Terms:
Awarded to Chief Petty Officers, Petty Officers and Men of the Navy (or Army/Air Force personnel of equal rank serving with the fleet) who show themselves to the fore in action, and set an example of bravery and resource under fire but without performing acts of such pre-eminent bravery as would render them eligible for the Conspicuous Gallantry Medal.

Bars:
For additional acts of bravery. (Laurelled Silver bar).

Obverse:
1. George VI, crowned head, facing left.
2. Elizabeth II, crowned head, facing right.

Reverse:
Inscription in three lines: FOR / DISTINGUISHED / SERVICE within a wreath of laurel and surmounted by the crown.

Description:
Circular, 1.42 inches, silver.

Mounting:
Straight suspender with single toe claw and inward scroll claws.

Ribbon:
1¼ inches; Dark Blue—White—Dark Blue of equal width with a narrow Dark Blue stripe down the centre of the white.

Dates:
Instituted 14 October 1914.

Issued:
George VI - 114 + 2 First Bars; Elizabeth II - 2.

Examples:
C.P.O. Albert Leo Bonner, D.S.M., B.E.M., R.C.N. — H.M.C.S. Nootka 20/12/52
Canada Gazette, 13 June 1953, page 1713. Her majesty the QUEEN has been graciously pleased to award the following decoration to personnel in HMC ships, for service in Korean waters: The Distinguished Service Medal; Petty Officer Second Class G.E. Jamieson, RCN, 5161-H
"On 2nd October, 1952, an enemy shell struck the ship in the quarters where he was serving as gun captain. Although several of his men were killed or wounded, by his example of courage and coolness, he rallied the gun crews and kept the guns in action. His outstanding bravery and leadership inspired the men serving under him."

30. MILITARY MEDAL

Terms:

Awake to Warrant Officers, NCOs and Men for individual or associated acts of bravery and devotion under fire on the recommendation of a Commander-in-Chief in the Field.

Bars:

For additional acts of bravery. (Laurelled Silver Bar)

Obverse:

1. George V, uncrowned head, in Field Marshall's uniform, facing left.
2. George VI, crowned head, facing left.
3. Elizabeth II, crowned head, facing right.

Reverse:

Inscription in four lines: FOR / BRAVERY / IN THE / FIELD encircled by a laurel wreath and surmounted by the Royal Cypher and Crown.

Description:

Circular, 1.42 inches, silver.

Mounting:

Ornate scroll suspender with single toe claw and inward scroll claws.

Ribbon:

1¼ inches; Dark Blue edges (¼"), White—Red—White—Red—White center stripes each ⅛" wide.

Dates:

Instituted 25 March 1916.

Issued:

WWI — 12,345 + 838 First Bars + 37 Second Bars
WWII — 1,255 + 10 First Bars + 1 Second Bar
Korea — 53 (made up of 29 George VI medals & 24 EIIR medals)

Examples:

Cpl. C.M. Anderson, M.M. — Seaforth Highlanders — 22 May 1944, his section was under the sniper fire of an 88 mm gun. He tried unsuccessfully several times to locate the sniper and draw his fire. He finally succeeded, killing the sniper but was wounded in the process. He continued on, eventually charging a machine gun post and killing its occupants.

Gunner K.W. Wishart, M.M. — 2nd R.C.H.A. — 28 May 1952, during an R.C.R. attack against the hill-encircled village of Chail-li, Korea, he was the wireless operator for the forward observation officer. Under heavy enemy fire from surrounding hills, Wishart stood by his set, transmitting orders for the concentrations which eventually broke up the Chinese counter-effort and covered the Canadian withdrawal.

Terms:

Awarded to non-commissioned officers and men for an act or acts of exceptional valour, courage or devotion to duty whilst flying in active operations against the enemy.

Bars:

For additional acts of bravery. (Bars as for DFC) (None to Canadians)

Obverse:

1. George V, uncrowned coinage head, facing left.
2. George VI, uncrowned coinage head, facing left.

Reverse:

Within a wreath of laurel, a representation of Athena Nike seated on an aeroplane, a hawk rising from her right arm above the words FOR COURAGE.

Description:

Oval, $1^3/8$ inches by $1^5/8$ inches, silver.

Mounting:

A bomb attached to the clasp and ribbon by two wings.

Ribbon:

$1^1/4$ inches; Violet and White alternate bars, $^1/16$ inches wide at a 45° angle left to right. (until July 1919 the bars were horizontal).

Dates:

Instituted 3 June 1918.

Issued:

George V — 1; George VI — 516

Examples:

George "Buzz" Beurling, D.S.O., D.F.C., D.F.M. & Bar. — on 6 July 1942 he hit an Italian Cant bomber, shot down two Italian Macchi fighters and shot down a Messerschmitt and was awarded the DFM — at this time he was a Sergeant in the RAF and later transferred to the RCAF.

Flt. Sgt. S.R. Cole, DFM (radio operator) and Flt. Sgt. I.J. Bodnoff DFM were aboard Flt. Lt. David Hornell's Canso on 24 June 1944 when they sank a German U-Boat but were shot down in the process. The crew spent 24 hours in the cold Atlantic before being rescued. Hornell received the Victoria Cross, Cole & Bodnoff the DFM, F/O Bernard Denomy the D.S.O., F/O S.E. Matheson and F/O Graham Campbell the D.F.C. and Sgt. Scott and Sgt. Fernand St. Laurent (who both died) were mentioned in dispatches. RCAF Squadron 162.

32. AIR FORCE MEDAL

Terms:
Awarded to non-commissioned officers and men for an act or acts of exceptional valour, courage or devotion to duty whilst flying, though not in active operations against the enemy.

Bars:
For additional acts of bravery. (Bar as to DFC - none to Canadians)

Obverse:
1. George V, uncrowned coinage head, facing left.
2. George VI, uncrowned coinage head, facing left.
3. Elizabeth II, uncrowned coinage head, facing right.

Reverse:
Within a laurel, a representation of Hermes, mounted on a hawk in flight bestowing a wreath. The date 1918 is behind Hermes on the George VI and Elizabeth II medals.

Description:
Oval, 1$^3/_8$ inches by 1$^5/_8$ inches, silver.

Mounting:
Bomb attached to the clasp and ribbon by two wings.

Ribbon:
1$^1/_4$ inches; Red and White alternate stripes, $^1/_{16}$" wide at a 45° angle left to right. (until July 1919 the bars were horizontal)

Dates:
Instituted 3 June 1918.

Issued:
WWI (George V) — 1 (Sgt. Maj. Walter Robert Maxwell)
WWII (George VI) — 43 + 3 to Canadians in the RAF (F/Sgts. Bishop, Hornby, Reilley)
1948 (George VI) — 1 (Cpl. J.P. Rae)
1951 (George VI) — 1 (Sgt. George Brown Leckie, RCAF Stn. Edmonton)
1952 (EIIR) — 1 (F/Sgt. A.A. Drackley, for the Korean airlift)
1953 (EIIR) — 1 (Cpl. G.R. Reed, for the Korean airlift)

Example:
Sergeant John Bell McRae, RCAF No. 1 Bombing School was pilot on an Anson which was hit by another Anson and had a third of his left wing destroyed. He flew the aircraft to an area to allow his two bomb aimers to parachute to safety and then made a successful wheels-up landing at his home base. (1944)

33.   CONSPICUOUS GALLANTRY MEDAL   C.G.M.

Terms:

A. Navy: Awarded to CPOs, POs, and Men of the Navy (and in WWII to NCOs and Men of the Army/Air Force serving with the fleet or serving afloat, eg. Air/Sea rescue operations) who may at any time distinguish themselves by acts of pre-eminent bravery in action against the enemy.

B. Flying: Awarded to WOs, NCOs, and Men of the Air Forces and Military for acts of conspicuous gallantry whilst flying in active operations against the enemy. (instituted in January 1943).

Bars:

For additional acts of bravery (none to Canadians).

Obverse:

1. George VI, crowned head, facing left.

Reverse:

Inscription in 3 lines: FOR / CONSPICUOUS / GALLANTRY within a wreath of laurel and surmounted by a crown.

Description:

Circular, 1.42 inches, silver. (Navy & Air Force medals identical).

Mounting:

Straight suspender with single toe claw with inward scrolls on rim.

Ribbons:

A. Navy — 1¼ inches; White with Dark Blue (³/₈") edges.
B. Air Force — 1¼ inches; Light Blue with Dark Blue (³/₈") edges.

Dates:

Instituted 7 July 1874; Air Force medal introduced 15 January 1943.

Issued:

NAVY (WWII — George VI) — 2
   (A/PO M.L. Bernays, RCNR; AS M.R. Kerwin, RCNVR)
AIR FORCE (WWII — George VI) — 13 (plus 3 RAF serving with the RCAF)

Examples:

Sgt. J.C. Bailey (62 Sqn); F/Sgt. K.W. Brown (617 Sqn); Sgt. W.H. Cardy (427 Sqd), F/Sgt. J.C. Cooke (103 Sqd); F/Sgt. W.E. Crabe (170 Sqn); Sgt. P. Englebrecht (424 Sqd); F/Sgt. A.W.J. Larden (L.G. 24 Sept. 43); F/Sgt. R.B. Maxwell (428 Sqd); Sgt. G.W. Meadows (166 Sqd); WO R.J. Meek (626 Sqd); F/Sgt. J.V. Russell (15 Sqd); Sgt. L.F. Williamson (428 Sqd).

Terms:

Introduced in 1917 as part of the Order of the British Empire for those who have rendered important services to the Empire. In 1918, a military division was created for all commissioned, warrant and subordinate officers of the military services.

In 1922, the medal was divided into the Medal of the Most Excellent Order of the British Empire for Gallantry (known as the E.G.M., Empire Gallantry Medal) and the Medal of the Most Excellent Order of the British Empire for Meritorious Service (B.E.M.). The E.G.M. was superceded by the George Cross in September 1940.

The B.E.M. continued to be awarded for meritorious service after 1940 but also for gallantry. A military & civilian divisions continued.

Bars:

Awarded for additional acts of gallantry (silver laurelled bar). After 1957, a silver emblem of two oak leaves was awarded with the medal when it was awarded for gallantry. The oak leaves would also be worn on the ribbon in undress. In undress, the recipient of a bar wears a rosette. (no bars to Canadians but oak leaves have been).

Obverse:

Britannia seated with sun to her right. Legend around the edge reads FOR GOD AND THE EMPIRE and in exergue (below) is the inscription FOR MERITORIOUS SERVICE. The E.G.M. had FOR GALLANTRY in exergue.

Reverse:

Royal Cypher surmounted by a crown with the words: INSTITUTED BY / KING GEORGE V within a border of four heraldic lions.

Description:

Circular, 1.42 inches, silver. A thin medal.

Mounting:

A straight clasp attached to the medal by laurel leaves.

Ribbon:

1917-37: 1-$^1/_{16}$ inches; Purple (military had a central thin Red stripe)
1937 on: 1$^1/_4$ inches; Rose Pink edged with thin pearl grey stripes. Military has central thin grey stripe added.

Dates:

Instituted in August 1917; amended 1922; amended 1940; amended 1957.

Issued:

Pre WWII	unknown		
WWII	approx.	1200	(387 to the RCAF)
Korea	Army	21	(4 George VI + 17 EIIR)
	RCN	4	(1 George VI + 3 EIIR)
	RCAF	2	(2 EIIR; F/Sgt. A.L. Engelbert & Cpl. J.B. Trudel)

Military (Gallantry)

1951	RCAF	1	(George VI — Sgt. D. Wright)
1952	RCAF	1	(EIIR — Sgt. LAC R.B. Gelinas)
1953	Army	1	(EIIR — Sgt. A.W. Graham, Toronto Scottish)
1955	RCN	1	(AS J.R. Grenier)
1958	RCAF	1	(A/Sgt. I.J. McPherson, CD)
1963	RCAF	1	(LAC R.G. Cole)
1964	RCAF	3	(Cpl. G.W. Snider, CD; LAC H.F. Schulz; Cpl. P.E. Blank, CD)
1965	RCN	1	(AS D.V. Patterson)
1967	RCN	2	(LS D.C. White & AS W.T. Gray, HMCS Nipigon)
1967	RCAF	1	(Cpl. G.J. Metka, CD)

Civil Division for Gallantry: 1958 — 1; 1965 — 3; 1966 — 2; 1968 — 5
Civil Division for Merit : 1951 to 1968 — 10

35. EMPIRE GALLANTRY MEDAL   E.G.M.

Terms:

From 1922 until 1940, the Medal of the Order of the British Empire, for Gallantry, was known as the E.G.M. The British Empire Medal was awarded for service and the Empire Gallantry Medal for gallantry.

Obverse:

Same as B.E.M. except the words for gallantry in exergue. Remainder of medal and ribbon is as described for the British Empire Medal.

Dates:

1922 to 1940; superceded by the George Cross (EGMs converted to G.C.s)

Example:

AC1 Ernest Frost, RCAF, won the EGM when he rescued an unconscious pilot from a burning aircraft that had collided with another on takeoff. The EGM was converted to a George Cross 24 Sept. 1940 (presented 21 Oct. 40).

Terms:

There are four Albert Medals awarded for Gallantry:

a) A.M. (first class) in Gold for Gallantry in saving life at sea;

b) A.M. (second class) for Gallantry in saving life at sea (in bronze);

c) A.M. (first class) in Gold for Gallantry in saving life on land, and;

d) A.M. (second class) for Gallantry in saving life on land (in bronze).

The standard of gallantry was very high in that the recipient's risk of death had to be greater than his chances of survival and, in the case of the gold medals, the risk had to be altogether exceptional. The gold medal was replaced in 1949 with the George Cross and the bronze medal only awarded posthumously. The bronze medal was discontinued in 1971.

Obverse:

a) a gold oval-shaped badge enamelled in dark blue, with a Monogram composed of the letters V and A interlaced with an Anchor erect in gold, surrounded with a Garter in Bronze, inscribed in raised letters of gold: FOR GALLANTRY IN SAVING LIFE AT SEA. Surmounted by Prince Consort's crown.

b) as above but in bronze & dark blue enamel.

c) as above but enamelled in crimson and gold, no anchor and the words: FOR GALLANTRY IN SAVING LIFE ON LAND.

d) as for (c) but in bronze with crimson enamel.

Reverse:

Plain.

Description:

Oval, 1½" by 1¼", in gold or bronze, with blue or crimson enamel.

Mounting:

Ring attached to top part of the crown.

Ribbon:

1⅜ inches;

a) White with five ⅛" stripes of Dark Blue

b) White with thin Dark Blue edges and a central Dark Blue stripe (⁵/₁₆").

c) White with five ⅛" stripes of Crimson. (Crimson at each edge).

d) White with thin Crimson edges and a central Crimson stripe (⁵/₁₆").

Dates:

1866 (sea); 1877 (land); gold ended 1949; bronze ended 1971.

26 to Canadians

Examples:
Edward Bell — saved 7 lives in a forest fire 11 July 1911 — his medal in bronze was for sale for $5500.00 in January 1982.
The last Canadian Albert Medal was awarded 4 August 1956 (Posthumously) to Sub-Lieutenant Arthur Latimer Corscadden, Royal Candian Sea Cadet Corps Ark Royal who lost his life trying to save a sea cadet when a whaler overturned on Lake Ontario. "The gallant action of this junior officer is in keeping with the highest traditions of the Royal Canadian Navy."

37. EDWARD MEDAL   E.M.

Terms:
A 1st Class (silver) and 2nd Class (Bronze) medal was awarded to those saving or endeavouring to save the lives of others from perils in Mines and Quarries who have endangered their own lives. The award was amended to include gallantry in industry. No bars to Canadians.

Obverse:
a) Edward VII, uncrowned, facing left.
b) George V, uncrowned, facing left.

Reverse:
Mines: A miner rescuing a comrade with the words FOR COURAGE.
Industry: Female figure holding a wreath with an industrial town in the background and near the bottom the words: FOR (figure) COURAGE.

Description:
Circular, 1.42 inches, in silver or bronze.

Mounting:
Oval ring (⁹/₁₆" wide) on a small mounting.

Ribbon:
1³/₈ inches; Dark Blue with ³/₁₆" Yellow edges (edges corded).

Dates:
1907 (Mines); 1909 (industry); silver medal discontinued 1949.

Issued:
5 G.H. Lamb 1907 (Class I - p); A.H. Adcock 1911 (Class II);
Wm. McFall 1911 (Class I - p); J.R. Roderick 1915 (Class II);
Leo Patrick Powell 1915 (Class II) — none to Canadians since.

38. MILITARY GENERAL SERVICE MEDAL (1793-1814)

Terms:
Awarded to any rank present at any battle commemorated and who applied for the medal. In all, 29 bars were awarded to this British medal with the three listed below being given to Canadians for action in Canada.

Bars:
a) FORT DETROIT — 16 August 1813, Brigadier-General Isaac Brock attacked Fort Detroit and the garrison surrendered.
b) CHATEAUGUAY — 26 October 1813, the Americans tried to capture Montreal but were surprised by a British force under command of LCol. Charles de Salaberry and the Americans were routed.
c) CHRYSTLER'S FARM — 11 November 1813, the Americans again tried to capture Montreal, but this time were defeated at Chrystler's Farm by a force led by LCol. Morrison. Thus ended the American invasion of Lower Canada.

Obverse:
Queen Victoria, diademed bust, facing left, with 1848 below the bust.

Reverse:
Queen Victoria standing on a dias with a wreath of laurel, crowning the Duke of Wellington who kneels before her on his left knee. A lion crouches beside the dias. Around the top half of the circumference is the inscription, TO THE BRITISH ARMY while in exergue is 1793 - 1814.

Description:
Circular, 1.42 inches, silver.

Mounting:
Plain, straight swivelling suspender with double toe claw.

Ribbon:
1¼ inches; Crimson with Dark Blue border stripes (⅛" wide).

Dates:
Authorized 1 June 1847; (34 years after the events commemorated).

Issued:
320 - Fort Detroit Bars; 338 - Chateauguay Bars; 233 - Chrystler' Farm Bars; 24 - Multiples Bars.

Example:
J.B. Lapierre, Canadian Militia - only winner of all three bars.

39. CANADIAN GENERAL SERVICE MEDAL (1866 - 1870)

Terms:

Awarded to members of the Imperial and Canadian Forces which had taken part in the suppression of the Fenian Raids and Riel's First Rebellion, the latter generally referred to as the Red River Expedition.

Bars:

a) FENIAN RAID 1866 - Fenians is the name of the old Irish National Militia. Following the Civil War in the U.S.A., the American Fenians were bolstered by civil war mercenaries. Needing something to occupy this large force with, John O'Neil crossed the Niagara River to invade Canada making his headquarters at Limeridge. At Ridgeway, the Fenians defeated a force of Canadian Militia but withdrew to the U.S.A. when a stronger force was sent from Canada. President Johnson had many of the Fenians arrested.

b) FENIAN RAID 1870 - 26 May 1870, O'Neil again crossed the border but was quickly forced back and again arrested by the Americans.

c) RED RIVER 1870 - Colonel Garnet Wolseley led an expedition to Fort Garry leaving Toronto on 14 May and reaching Fort Garry on 24 August. They captured Louis Riel and prevented a Fenian raid on Manitoba.

Obverse:

Queen Victoria, diademed and veiled bust, wearing the Order of the Garter, facing left. Legend: VICTORIA REGINA ET IMPERATRIX.

Reverse:

Red ensign of Canada floating with the breeze surrounded by a wreath of maple leaves and surmounted by a ribbon on a scroll bearing the word: CANADA.

Description:

Circular, 1.42 inches, silver.

Mounting:

Plain, straight swivelling suspender with double toe claw.

Ribbon:

1 1/4 inches; Red - White - Red in three equal stripes. (same ribbon as proposed for the 1943 Canada Medal)

Dates:

Authorized January 1899 (29 years after the last event commemorated).

Issued:

17,635 (15,300 to Canadian units); Always with bars.

1866 Fenian Raid, 11,221; 1870 Fenian Raid, 4,510; 1870 Red River, 350; 1866 & 1870 Fenian Raids, 1,411; 1866 Fenian Raid & Red River, 105; 1870 Fenian Raid & Red River, 15; All 3 bars, 23.

40. EGYPT MEDAL (1884-1885)

Terms:

Awarded to members of the Army and Navy who took part in the Egyptian Campaigns between 1882 and 1889. The medal has 13 bars and was also awarded without a bar. Canadian Boatmen were awarded the medal with THE NILE 1884-85 bar and some received the KIRBEKAN bar.

Bars:

a) THE NILE 1884-85; Awarded to those who served south of Assouan on or before 7 March 1885 as part of the expedition to relieve General Gordon who was under seige at Kartoum. (Canadian Boatmen included).

b) KIRBEKAN: Awarded to those members of the expedition to relieve Gordon who actually reached Khartoum. This bar was only awarded with the above bar.

Obverse:

Queen Victoria, diademed and veiled bust, facing left, with the inscription VICTORIA REGINA ET IMPERATRIX (same as North West Canada).

Reverse:

The Sphinx on a pedestal with the word EGYPT above. No date in exergue on Canadian medals. (earlier medals have 1882 in exergue).

Description:

Circular, 1.42 inches, silver.

Mounting:

Plain, straight swivelling suspender with double toe claw.

Ribbon:

1¼ inches; Blue-White-Blue-White-Blue in 5 equal stripes.

Dates:

Authorized 1 September 1885; Engraved with number, name & contingent.

Issued:

371 (all with THE NILE 1884-85 bar; 45 also have bar KIRBEKAN).

Example:

T. Allard, Three Rivers Contingent (bar THE NILE 1884-85)

41. KHEDIVE'S BRONZE STAR

Terms:
The Khedive (ruler) of Egypt, Tewfik Mahommed awarded this medal to all who were awarded the Soudan Medal. One bar only and none to Canadians.

Obverse:
An annulus with the legend EGYPT 1884-6 above and Arabic inscription below and in the centre is the head of the Sphinx with three pyramids behind. (Awarded Canadian Boatmen—three other obverses issued with dates a) 1882; b) 1884; c) Star undated).

Reverse:
Crown surmounted by a Star and Crecent and the letters TM interlaced.

Description:
Star shaped with 5 points; $1^7/_8$ inches across; bronze.

Mounting:
A small ring is attached to the medal between the top two points. On the ornamented bronze bar is a Crescent with a star in the middle of the crescent. At the bottom of the Crescent is another small ring. These two rings are joined by a third ring.

Ribbon:
$1^1/_2$ inches; Dark Blue

Dates:
Authorized 5 November 1884; Issued unnamed.

Issued:
312 (384 were entitled to the Soudan Medal & Khedive's Star).

Example:
221 Boatman G. Harris, Ottawa Contingent

42. PONTIFICAL ZOUAVES VOLUNTEER MEDAL (1869 - 1870)

Terms:
Issued to Canadian volunteers who were members of the French Battalion of Zouaves who fought in the Italian campaign in 1869-1870.

Obverse:
Bust of Pope Leo XIII, facing left with legend: LEO XIII PONT. MAX.

Reverse:
Legend in two lines: BENE / MERENTI.

Description:
Large ring at top of medal attaches to bottom of bar with ROMA on it.

Ribbon:
1¼ inches; 5 equal bars of light blue and white.

Dates:
Authorized 10 March 1891.

Issued:
150 to Canadians (507 were eligible).

Examples:
Louis Caron of Rimouski, Quebec.
Charles Collin, of Longueuil.

43. NORTH WEST CANADA MEDAL

Terms:
Awarded originally to each soldier taking part in the suppression of the Riel Rebellion of 1885. Only those who served west of Port Arthur were awarded the medal. The NWMP were excluded until 1900 when the medals were extended to members of the NWMP who served in the campaign. A grant of 320 acres of land and script of $80 was also awarded.

Bars:
SASKATCHEWAN — Awarded
to all who took part in any or all three main encounters during the rebellion (those along the Saskatchewan River, Fish River and the battle at Batoche).

(BATOCHE) — Medals are found with unofficial bars for Batoche.

Obverse:
Queen Victoria, diademed and veiled bust, facing left (same as Soudan).

Reverse:
The legend in three lines: NORTH WEST / 1885 / CANADA within a wreath of maple leaves.

Description:
Circular, 1.42 inches, silver.

Mounting:
Plain, straight swivelling suspender with double toe claw.

Ribbon:
1 1/4 inches; Slate Gray (Blue) with 1/2" Crimson stripe 1/8" from edge.

Dates:
Authorized 24 July 1885 for issue 18 Sept. 1885. (Issued unnamed).

Issued:
5,650 including 1,753 with SASKATCHEWAN bar.

Example:
General Middleton, Canadian Commander.

44. QUEEN'S SOUTH AFRICA MEDAL

Terms:
Awarded to all troops who actually served in South Africa between 11 October 1899 and 31 May 1902 (Boer War).

Bars:
Twenty-six bars; common ones to Canadians: CAPE COLONY, ORANGE FREE STATE, JOHANNESBURG, BELFAST, TRANSVAAL, NATAL, DRIEFONTEIN, SOUTH AFRICA 1901, SOUTH AFRICA 1902.

Obverse:
Queen Victoria, crowned and veiled bust in ceremonial robes, facing left.

Reverse:
Britannia holding the Union Flag in her left hand and a laurel wreath in her right hand. In the right background are troops marching to the

coast and in the left background are two Men-of-War. Around the top are the words: SOUTH AFRICA. The first medals awarded to the Lord Strathcona's Horse bore the dates 1899-1900 but the dates were taken off subsequent medals as war went beyond 1900.

Description:
Circular, 1.42 inches, silver.

Mounting:
Plain, straight swivelling suspender with double toe claw.

Ribbon:
1 1/4 inches; Orange centre (1/2"), Dark Blue & Red stripes (red at edge).

Dates:
1901; engraved with Number, Rank, Name and Regiment.

Issued:
3,860 (including 50 with dates to the Lord Strathcona Horse)

Examples:
4 Victoria Cross winners
Sergeant A.H.L. Richardson, V.C. Lord Strathcona's Horse
Lieutenant H.Z.C. Cockburn, V.C. Royal Canadian Dragoons
Lieutenant E.J.G. Holland, V.C. Royal Canadian Dragoons
Lieutenant E.W. Turner, V.C. D.S.O., Royal Canadian Dragoon (later rose to the rank of Lieutenant General and awarded KCB, KCMG).

45. KING'S SOUTH AFRICA MEDAL

Terms:

Awarded to all troops who served in South Africa on or after 1 Jan. 1902 and who would complete 18 months service before 1 June 1902. This medal was never issued alone but always in conjunction with the Queen's Medal.

Bars:

SOUTH AFRICA 1901 — for service in 1901 towards the 18 months required.
SOUTH AFRICA 1902 — for those who served in 1902.

Obverse:

Edward VII, in Field Marshall's uniform, facing left.

Reverse:

As for Queen's South Africa Medal (no dates).

Description:

Circular, 1.42 inches, silver.

Mounting:

Plain, straight swivelling suspender with double toe claw.

Ribbon:

1 1/4 inches; three equal stripes Green-White-Orange (light green first).

Dates:

Authorized 1 October 1902; engraved with Number, Rank, Name & Regiment.

Issued:

160 (to Canadians)

Examples:

Major C. Ross, D.S.O. - Canadian Scouts
Major A. Hodgins, - 2nd Canadian Mounted Rifles.

Note:

Approximately 200 more Canadians would have received this medal because they returned to South Africa for a second time but due to the long sea voyages, they did not get the required 18 months service. Those Canadians who did receive the medal usually remained in South Africa transferring between units (eg. LSH to Cdn Scouts to the SAC or RCA to 2 CMR to Cdn Scouts)   CMR — Canadian Mounted Rifles

WORLD WAR ONE MEDALS

46. 1914 STAR

Terms:

Awarded to all officers, non-commissioned officers and men of the British and Indian Expeditionary Forces including civilian medical practitioners, nursing sisters, nurses and others employed with military hospitals, who actually served in France or Belgium on the establishment of a unit of the British Expeditionary Forces, between 5 August 1914 and midnight of the 22/23 November 1914. Not awarded for service afloat. It is often called the 'Mons Star'.

Bar:

5th Aug. 22nd Nov: 1914 — The bar was awarded to those who actually served under fire or were present on duty within range of the enemy mobile artillery in France or Belgium between the above dates and on the strength of units and formations contained in the official lists.

Obverse:

In the centre, on a scroll, is the date '1914'; above the date on a scroll is the month AUG and below the date on a scroll is the month Nov. These three scrolls are surrounded by a laurel wreath $^3/_4$ inches in diameter and on the bottom of the wreath is superscribed G V.

Reverse

Plain with the recipients number, rank, name and unit — only Canadian 1914 Stars have 2-STA.HOSP.C.A.M.C. for the unit.

Description:

A bronze star measuring $1^3/_4$ inches wide and $2^1/_2$ inches top to bottom. The star has three points with the uppermost point being replaced by a crown. Across the face are two crossed swords (handles at bottom), the points and handles of which protrude and thus form four additional points.

Mounting:

The ring for suspension is stamped out solid with the piece and is attached at the top point of the crown.

Ribbon:

$1^1/_4$ inches; watered and shade left to right, Red-White-Blue. The recipient of the bar wears a small silver rosette on the ribbon in undress.

Issued:

160 to Canadians of the 2nd Canadian Stationary Hospital all without bars plus a few others to Canadians with British units. (378,000 medals plus approximately 145,000 bars awarded in total).

47.   1914 — 1915 STAR

Terms:
Awarded to all who saw service in any theatre of war against the central powers between 5th August, 1914 and 31 December 1915 except those eligible for the 1914 Star. Canada considered "overseas" to be service beyond the three mile limit and consequently many RCN small ships were entitled to this star.

Bar:
Nil

Obverse:
In the centre, on a scroll, is the date 1914-15. The scroll is surrounded by a laurel wreath and on the bottom is the Royal Cypher G V (v inside a large G).

Reverse:
Plain with the recipients number, rank, name and unit. Units include the following engravings: 1/CAN : INF : 1/CAN.MTD : RIF :, 2/CAN.MTD : RIF :, 3/CAN.MTD : RIF :, 5/CAN.MTD : RIF :, R.CAN : R., P.P.C.L.I. R.CAN : DNS :, LD : S'CONA'SH., F.GH., R.C.H.A., CAN : A.M.C., CAN : A.S.C., CAN : FD : ART :, CAN : Y.M.C.A., E.E., 1/CAN : DIV. CYCLIST., 1/CAN : DIV : CAV :, 1/CAN : INF : BDE : H.Q., 2/CAN : INF : BDE : H.Q., /CAN : D.S.COY, 2/CAN : DIV : A.C., 1/CAN : DIV : AC., H.M.C.S. NIOBE, H.M.C.S. GLORENCE, H.M.C.S. RAINBOW, H.M.C.S. EARL GREY.

As per 1914 Star.

Mounting:
As per 1914 Star.

Ribbon:
As per 1914 Star (1 1/4"; watered & shaded Red-White-Blue).

Issued:
71,150 to the C.E.F. (2,366,000 approximately issued in total).

Example:
Cdr. Henry Beattie Bell - Irving, D.S.C. & Bar (medals on display in Wardroom, H.M.C.S. Discovery).

48. BRITISH WAR MEDAL

Terms:

Awarded to all ranks of the Overseas Military Forces of Canada who came overseas from Canada between 5 August 1914 and 11 November 1918 or who have served in a theatre of war. Those who enlisted in the O.M.F.C. in the United Kingdom and have not served in a theatre of war are not entitled to this medal. The R.A.F. requirement was the same as the Army but the personnel of the naval forces required 28 days of

mobilized service or if they lost their lives before the service period was complete. Seamen of the Canadian Merchant Marine who served at sea not less than 6 months and crews of Dominion Government Ships and the Canadian Merchantile Marine were also eligible.

Bar:

Nil

Obverse:

George V, uncrowned coinage head, facing left, with the legend GEORGIVS V BRITT: OMN: REX ET IND: IMP:

Reverse:

A horseman (St. George, naked) armed with a short sword (an allegory of the physical and mental strength which achieves victory over Prussianism). The horse tramples on the Prussian shield and the skull and cross-bones. In the upper circumference between the horses neck and the knee of the rider is the sun of Victory; in right and left field is 1914 and 1918.

Description:

Circular, 1.42 inches, silver (Bronze to Chinese, Maltese & native Labour Corps).

Mounting:

Plain, straight, non-swivelling suspender with single toe claw.

Ribbon:

1 1/4 inches; Orange centre ($^5/_8$"); edges from outside to inside are Blue-Black-White ($^1/_8$", $^1/_{16}$", $^1/_8$" wide). Orange is watered.

Dates:

Authorized 26 July 1919 (for service 5 August 1914 - 11 November 1918).

Issued:

427,993 to Canadians in the C.E.F. (6,500,000 in total were awarded).

49. VICTORY MEDAL (INTER-ALLIED WAR MEDAL)

Terms:
Awarded to all officers, warrant officers, NCOs and men of the fighting forces and civilians under contract, and others employed with military hospitals who actually served on the establishment of a unit in a theatre of war between 5 August 1914 and midnight 11/12 November 1918. (It was also issued to members of a British Naval mission to Russia 1919-1920 and for mine clearance in the North Sea between 11 November 1918 and

30 November 1919). This medal is never issued alone but is always issued with the British War Medal.

Bars:
Nil — Those Mentioned in Dispatches wear an oak leaf on the ribbon.

Obverse:
The winged, full-length figure of Victory, with her left arm extended and holding a palm branch in her right hand.

Reverse:
The legend in four lines: THE GREAT / WAR FOR / CIVILIZATION / 1914 - 1919 with a line of dots below the words surrounded by a wreath.

Description:
Circular, 1.42 inches, copper lacqured bronze.

Mounting:
A ½ inch diameter ring which passes through a loop fixed to the top of the medal. Ring will move forwards and backwards but not sideways.

Ribbon:
1½ inches; watered, double rainbow from the outside to the middle Violet - Blue - Green - Yellow - Orange centre.

Date:
Authorized 1919 (for service 5 August 1914 - 11 November 1918).

Naming:
BWM and VM were inscribed with the highest recorded rank: the Number, Rank, Name and Unit indented on the edge except officers do not have their unit. The Units include all those listed for the Stars plus: 1-CND.INF. numbers 38, 43, 44, 46, 47, 50, 52, 54, 58, 60, 72, 73, 75, 78, 87, 102, 116; 1-C.M.R., 2-C.M.R, 4-C.M.R., 5-C.M.R., R.C.R., R.CD., P.P.C.L.I., L.S.H.-R.C., F.G.H., C.L.H., R.C.N., R.N.C.V.R., R.A.F., F.F.C., R.N.A.S., CAN CAV.BDE., C.A.M.C., C.E., C.A.S.C., C.F.A., C.F.C., C.R.T., C.A.G.S., C.S.E.F., C.A.V.C., C.G.A., C.M.G.BDE., R.C.H.A., C.M.R., CAN.PNR.BN., CAN.INF.WKS.COY., R.NEWF'fd., CAN.LAB.BN.

50. MERCHANTILE MARINE WAR MEDAL (World War 1)

Terms:

Awarded to men who received the British War Medal and in addition served at sea on a least one voyage through a danger zone. It was also given to those who had served at sea for not less than six months between the 4 August 1914 and 11 November 1918. No bars.

Obverse:

George V, uncrowned coinage head, facing left.

Reverse:

Merchant ship ploughing her way through stormy seas; an enemy sub sinking and a sailing vessel are in the background. In exergue in three lines: FOR. WAR. SERVICE / MERCHANTILE. MARINE / .1914-1918. Raised wreath of laurel leaves is around the edge.

Description:

Circular, 1.42 inches, bronze.

Mounting:

Straight bar.

Ribbon:

1 1/4 inches; watered Green - thin White - Red

Dates:

Authorized Canada Gazette 8 May 1920

Total Issued:

624 to Canadians (134,333 in total)

WORLD WAR TWO STARS

Terms:
Described for each individual star. The Stars are authorized by Canadian Army Routine Order No. 6719, 16 August, 1946. For purposes of the awarding of a star, a period of one month is deemed to be 30 days. Service curtailed by death, or disability due to service, would qualify for the award. A recipient of a Decoration, Mention in Dispatches or a King's Commendation qualified for the award, irrespective of the length of service. Service spent in qualifying for one star could not run concurrently with service qualifying for another. Prisoner of War time could count towards the 39-45 Star but it would not count towards the earning of other stars unless the 39-45 Star time had been completed before capture.

Bars:
A bar to be sewn on the ribbon was awarded either as a special service connected with that star (1939-1945 Star & African Star) or to denote that the person qualified for the award of another specific star after the award of the first star. No more than five stars could be awarded to any individual. The Italy Star did not have any bars associated with it.

Obverse:
The Royal and Imperial Cypher (GRI with VI below it) is in the center, surmounted by a crown. The Cypher is surrounded by a circlet bearing the name of the particular star.

Reverse:
Plain — some individuals had their names engraved privately but no engraving was done on issue.

Description:
A six pointed star, 1 3/4 inches across the points and made of tombac (yellow copper, zinc alloy).

Ribbon:
1 1/4 inches wide. A silver rose emblem on the ribbon signified the award of a bar to the star. Ribbon colours are left to right.

51. THE 1939 — 1945 STAR

Terms:

6 months service on active operations. (2 months for active aircrew). between 2 September 1939 and 8 May 1945 for Europe or 2 September 1945 for the Pacific.

Bar:

BATTLE OF BRITAIN - awarded to members of the crews of fighter aircraft who took part in the Battle of Britain between 10 July and 31 October, 1940.

Total Issued:

305,000 (88 with bars)

Ribbon:

Dark Blue, Red and Light blue equal stripes. (Representing the Navy, Army and Air Force)

52. THE ATLANTIC STAR

Terms:

6 months service afloat between 3 September 1939 and 8 May 1945.

Bars:

FRANCE AND GERMANY if later entitled to this star.
AIR CREW EUROPE if later entitled to this star.

Total Issued:

43,500

Ribbon:

Blue, White and Sea-green stripes, shaded and watered. Representing the Atlantic Ocean.

53. THE AIR CREW EUROPE STAR

Terms:
2 months operational flying from the United Kingdom over Europe. between 3 September, 1939 and 5 June, 1944 (not awarded after D-Day)

Bars:
ATLANTIC if later entitled to this star. FRANCE AND GERMANY if later entitled to this star.

Total Issued:
12,800

Ribbon:
Light Blue with black edges and a narrow yellow stripe between the blue and black. (Representing continuous service by day and night)

54. THE AFRICA STAR

Terms:
Awarded for entry into an operational area of North Africa between 10 June, 1940 and 12 May, 1943. (one or more days service)

Bars:
FIRST ARMY for service with that army between 8 November 1942 and 12 May, 1943.

EIGHTH ARMY for service with that army between 23 October, 1942 and 12 May, 1943.

NORTH AFRICA 1942-1943 for service with the navy or Air Force between 23 October, 1942 and 12 May, 1943.

Total Issued:
7,400

Ribbon:
Pale Buff with a central Red stripe and two narrow stripes. Dark Blue at left and Light Blue at right. Representing the desert, the Navy, Army and Air Force. A 1 is worn on the ribbon for First Army bar, 8 for Eighth Army bar and rosette for North Africa.

55. THE PACIFIC STAR

Terms:
Awarded for operational service in the Pacific between 8 December, 1941 and 2 September, 1945

Bar:
BURMA if later entitled to that star.

Total Issued:
8,800

Ribbon:
Stripes of Red - narrow Dark Blue - Green - narrow Yellow (centre) - Green - narrow Light Blue - Red (Representing the forests and beaches and the Navy, Army and Air Force).

56. THE BURMA STAR

Terms:
Awarded for operational service in the Burma campaign between 11 December, 1941 and 2 September, 1945

Bar:
PACIFIC if later entitled to that star.

Total Issued:
5,500

Ribbon:
Red wide centre stripe with Dark Blue-Orange-Dark Blue edges. Red represents the Commonwealth Forces and Orange the sun.

57. THE ITALY STAR

Terms:
Awarded for operational service in Sicily or Italy between 11 June, 1943 and 8 May 1945.

Bar:
Nil

Total Issued:
91,000

Ribbon:
Alternate equal stripes Red — White — Green — White — Red. Colours represent the colours of Italy.

58. THE FRANCE AND GERMANY STAR

Terms:
Awarded for service in France, Belgium, Holland or Germany between 6 June, 1944 (D-Day) and 8 May 1945.

Bar:
ATLANTIC if later entitled to that star.
Note: The Aircrew Europe Bar was *NOT* issued with this star as one could not qualify for the Aircrew Europe Star after 5 June 1944.

Total Issued:
230,000

Ribbon:
Alternate equal stripes Blue — White — Red — White — Blue. (Representing the Union flag and those of France and the Netherlands but not Belgium).

WORLD WAR TWO MEDALS

59. THE DEFENCE MEDAL

Terms:
Awarded to Canadians for 6 months service in Britain between 3 September 1939 and 2 September 1945.

Bars:
Nil

Obverse:
George VI, uncrowned coinage head, facing left.

Reverse:
The Royal Crown resting on the stump of an oak tree and flanked by a lion and lioness. On the top left is the date 1939 and on the top right 1945. At the bottom is the wording: THE DEFENCE MEDAL.

Description:
Circular, 1.42 inches, silver 800 fine. British issues are made of cupro-nickel.

Mounting:
Plain, straight non-swivelling suspender with a single toe claw and claw supports on the rim with an inward scroll.

Ribbon:
1 1/4 inches; Orange (flame coloured) 1/2" central stripe flanked by 3/8" Light Green stripes with a narrow Black stripe in the middle of each green stripe. The Flame colour with green edges represents the enemy attacks on the green land of England and the black represents black-outs.

Dates:
Established 16 August 1945.

Issued:
325,000

60. CANADIAN VOLUNTEER SERVICE MEDAL

Terms:
Awarded to Canadians for 18 months voluntary service between 2 September 1939 and 2 Sept. 1945 or for any voluntary service outside Canada.

Bar:
Awarded for 60 days service outside of Canada. Silver bar with a maple leaf in the centre. A Silver Maple Leaf is worn on the ribbon in undress.

Obverse:
Seven Marching figures representing males and females of the Army, Air Force and Navy and the Nursing Service. Inscription around the edge reads: 1939 CANADA 1945 VOLUNTARY SERVICE VOLONTAIRE with a small maple leaf before and after the word SERVICE.

Reverse:
Coat of Arms of Canada.

Description:
Circular, 1.42 inches, silver 925 fine.

Mounting:
Small ring at top of medal with another passing through it and through a small hole in the straight suspender.

Ribbon:
1 1/4 inches; Royal Blue centre (1/2" wide) with two equal stripes of Scarlet and Green, the green being on the edge.

Dates:
Established 22 October 1943. Ribbon was issued during the war but the medal was not available until after the war.

Issued:
650,000 (525,500 with bar) - 1,183,000 were eligible for the medal.

61. THE 1939 - 1945 WAR MEDAL

Terms:
Awarded to all full-time personnel of the armed forces for 28 days service between 3 Sept. 1939 and 2 Sept. 1945. (also Merchant Navy).

Bar:
Nil - single oak leaf emblem is worn to signify a Mention in Despatches or King's Commendation for Brave Conduct or Valuable Service in the Air.

Obverse:
George VI, crowned head, facing left.

Reverse:
A Lion standing wanton on the body of a double headed dragon, the two heads, an eagle's and a dragon's signify the principal occidental and oriental enemies.

Description:
Circular, 1.42 inches, silver 800 fine (British issues cupro-nickel).

Mounting:
As per the Defence Medal.

Ribbon:
1 1/4 inches; White-Red-White narrow central stripes with 1/4" Dark Blue and Red stripes on the edge (red at the outer edge).

Dates:
Authorized 16 August 1946 (service between 2 Sept. 1939 - 2 Sept. 1945)

Issued:
700,000 including 4,450 to the Canadian Merchant Marine.

Note:
The medals awarded to the Canadian Merchant Marine and RCMP were officially named on the rim. (eg. Commander Dick Wilson)

62. CANADIAN KOREAN WAR MEDAL

Terms:

Awarded to Canadians for one day on the strength of an army unit in Korea; or, 28 days afloat; or, one sortie over Korea by the RCAF between 2 July 1950 and 27 July 1953.

Bar:

A single bronze oak leaf emblem is worn on the ribbon by those mentioned in dispatches. The RCN received 33 Mentions in Dispatches.

Obverse:

The uncrowned coinage head of Elizabeth II facing right with the legend ELIZABETH II DEI GRATIA REGINA around the edge and the word CANADA on the bottom of the legend.

Reverse:

The Hydra headed monster of Greek mythology being destroyed by Hercules with the word KOREA at the bottom.

Description:

Circular, 1.42 inches across, silver (800 fine) — British medal is in cupronickel and does not have CANADA at the bottom.

Mounting:

A scroll claw to a straight plain suspender and straight ribbon mount.

Naming:

Impressed capitals; regimental number and name.

Ribbon:

1 1/4 inches; Yellow-Blue-Yellow-Blue-Yellow in 5 equal stripes (1/4").

Dates:

2 July 1950 to 27 July 1953 (medal instituted in July 1951)

Total Issued:

15,000

Examples:

Cpl Ken Barwise, M.M., C.D. - 2 PPCLI (Military Medal at Kapyong)
Captain (N) Jeffry Vanstone Brock, D.S.O., D.S.C., C.D., RCN
CPO Albert Leo Bonner, D.S.M., B.E.M., RCN.
CPO George Vander-Haegen, D.S.M., B.E.M., RCN
Surgeon Lieutenant Chris Alfred West, RCN (M.I.D.)
Lieutenant (N), later VAdm. Andrew Collier, C.M.M., D.S.C., C.D. — H.M.C.S. Cayuga, D.S.C. awarded for leading the United Nations Naval Squadron through mine channels in December 1950. Collier was the navigator in Cayuga and Brock was the Commanding Officer.

63. UNITED NATIONS SERVICE MEDAL - KOREA (UNS Medal)

Terms:
The medal was earned for one day's service under United Nations command in Korea or the adjacent areas which included Japan and Okinawa. The medal could also be won for an aggregate of thirty days, which need not nave been consecutive, spent on official visits of inspections to the qualifying area. The qualifying period was 27 June 1950 to 27 July 1954 (one year longer than the other medal).

Bar:
Permanent Bar as part of the mount: KOREA or COREE on it.

Obverse:
Globe of the Earth seen from the North pole within a wreath of two olive branches (Emblem of the United Nations).

Reverse:
The inscription in 5 lines: FOR SERVICE IN / DEFENCE OF THE / PRINCIPLES OF THE / UNITED NATIONS or POUR LA DEFENSE / DES PRINCIPES DE / LA CHARTE DES / NATIONS UNIES.

Description:
Circular, 1³/₈ inches across, bronze alloy.

Mounting:
A scroll claw attaches to a straight plain suspender.

Naming:
Impressed; Regimental number and name.

Ribbon:
Alternate Blue and White; 17 stripes with blue on each edge.

Dates:
27 June 1950 to 27 July 1954 (instituted 12 December 1950)

Total Issued:
25,584 to Canadians (1,225,000 in total) - figures from the Director of Ceremonials in Ottawa as of 27 October 1981.

Examples:
Col. J.R. Stone, 2 PPCLI, Commanding Officer in Korea in 1951.
Brig. Gen. E.A.C. Amy, D.S.O., O.B.E., M.C., C.D.
Commander Robert Welland, D.S.C., C.D. (awarded bar to his D.S.C.)
Lieutenant (N) J.J. MacBrien, R.C.N. - awarded U.S.A. D.F.C.
Cdr. John Bovey, D.S.C., C.D. - awarded U.S.A.'s Bronze Star Medal

UNITED NATIONS MEDALS

Terms:
Described for each service. Medals are also awarded if the UN Force is terminated and the person was posted on strength and had physically reported to the Force. Medals are also awarded if service is terminated by death, injuries or other disability received while on duty with the UN Force and a certificate to this effect is given by the Commander.

Bar:
CONGO — When the first medals for service in the Congo were presented, the unique ONUC ribbon was not available. Therefore, the medals were presented using UNTSO ribbon (blue with white stripes near each edge) and a small (¹/₂ inch) bronze bar with the word CONGO was placed on the ribbon. UNTSO ribbon with the bar was to be worn only until the correct ONUC ribbon was available. Major-General Dupuis, Surgeon General, was one person who wore this bar for a short time. No other bars have been issued.

Obverse:
The United Nations Emblem surmounted by the letters: UN.
The UNEF medal had the UN emblem but had the letters: UNEF.
Reverse:
The inscription in two lines: IN THE SERVICE / OF PEACE.

Description:
Circular, 1.375 inches in diameter, bronze alloy.

Mounting:
Ball on top of the medal; loose ring (¹/₂") passes through hole in ball.

Ribbon:
Varies for each service; medal is the same for each service. 1³/₈".

Note:
In 1983, Canadians with more than one tour of service in the same UN operation were allowed to wear a small number on their ribbon in undress to signify multiple tours. Thus several Canadians wear a '2' or '3' and an occasional '4' on their Cyprus ribbon. The number is not shown when the medal is worn.

64. UNITED NATIONS EMERGENCY FORCE MEDAL-EGYPT   UNEF

Terms:
90 Days service: between 7 November 1956 & 19 May 1967.

Ribbon:
Sand Yellow with broad middle bar of UN Blue (a light blue). Two narrow stripes, outer Dark Blue and inner Dark Green are on the outer edges of the Sand stripes.

Issued:
9,963 to Canadians (58,031 in total)

65. UNITED NATIONS TRUCE SUPERVISION ORGANIZATION IN PALESTINE   UNTSO

Terms:
6 Months service: after 23 April 1948 — Current.

Ribbon:
UN Blue with a narrow White stripe near each edge.

Issued:
648 (to 31 March 1985) — 20 Canadians serving at any one time.

66. UNITED NATIONS OBSERVER GROUP IN LEBANON   UNOGIL

Terms:
30 Days service: between 11 June 1958 & 9 December 1958.

Ribbon:
UN Blue with a narrow White stripe near each edge. (same as UNTSO).

Issued:
77

67. UNITED NATIONS MILITARY OBSERVATION GROUP IN INDIA & PAKISTAN   UNMOGIP

Terms:
6 Months service: between 20 January 1948 & 20 January 1979.

Ribbon:
Dark Green centre merging outwards through shades of Lighter Green to White, with an abrupt break into UN Blue on the edges.

Issued:
501

68. ORGANISATIONS DES NATIONS UNIES AU CONGO
ONUC

Terms:
90 Days service: between 14 July 1960 & 30 June 1964.

Ribbon:
Dark Green centre with White border stripes and Dark Blue slevedges.

Issued;
1,900

69. UNITED NATIONS TEMPORARY EXECUTIVE AUTHORITY IN WEST NEW GUINEA
UNTEA

Terms:
90 Days service: between 1 October 1962 & 31 May 1963

Ribbon:
Dull Blue with Dark Green - White - Light Green narrow central stripes.

Issued:
13 to Canadians (91 in total)

70. UNITED NATIONS YEMEN OBSERVATION MISSION
UNYOM

Terms:
60 Days service: between 11 June 1963 & 4 September 1964.

Ribbon:
Dark Brown centre merging outwards through Lighter Brown shades to Sand Yellow with an abrupt break into UN Blue on the edges.

Issued:
30

71. UNITED NATIONS FORCE IN CYPRUS
UNFICYP

Terms:
90 Days service: after 27 March 1965 — Current.
30 Days service: between 27 March 1964 & 27 March 1965.

Ribbon:
UN Blue with wide central White stripe flanked by thin Dark Blue stripes.

Issued:
23,640 (to 31 March 1985) — approximately 515 Canadians on duty for each six month tour.

72. UNITED NATIONS INDIA — PAKISTAN OBSERVATION MISSION   UNIPOM

Terms:
90 Days service: between 22 September 1965 & 24 March 1966.

Ribbon:
Dark Green Centre merging outwards through shades of Lighter Green to White with an abrupt break into UN Blue on the edges (same as UN-MOGIP).

Issued:
112

73. UNITED NATIONS EMERGENCY FORCE MIDDLE EAST (2)   UNEFME

Terms:
90 Days service: between 26 October 1973 & 24 July 1979.

Ribbon:
Sand Yellow with two narrow Dark Blue stripes in the middle with UN Blue slevedges. ($^3/8$ inches).

Issued:
11,500 (1,145 at any one time).

74. UNITED NATIONS DISENGAGEMENT OBSERVER FORCE (GOLAN HEIGHTS)   UNDOF

Terms:
90 Days service: after 31 May 1974 — Current.

Ribbon:
Burgundy edges ($^3/8$"), UN Blue centre ($^5/16$") with thin Burgundy central stripe, thin Black stripes at each edge of the Blue and White stripes ($^1/8$") between the Black and Burgundy.

Issued:
4,110 (to 31 March 1985) — 220 Canadians serve at any one time.

Note:
UN and Commission Medals are authorized for wear by Canadians by individual Order in Council.

75. UNITED NATIONS INTERIM FORCE IN LEBANON
UNIFIL

Terms:
90 Days service: between 19 March 1978 & 6 October 1978.

Ribbon:
UN Blue - Bright Green - UN Blue in 3 equal stripes separated by thin stripes of Red-White-Red

Issued:
117

UNITED NATIONS MEDAL SUMMARY

FORMATION	SERVICE	COMMENCE-MENT	TERMINATE	ISSUED
UNS KOREA	1 Day	27 June 1950	27 July 1954	25,584
UNEF	90 Days	07 Nov. 1956	19 May 1967	9,963*
UNTSO	6 Months	23 April 1948	Current	648
UNOGIL	30 Days	11 June 1958	09 Dec. 1958	77
UNMOGIP	6 Months	20 Jan. 1948	20 Jan. 1979	501
ONUC	90 Days	14 July 1960	30 June 1964	1,900*
UNTEA	90 Days	01 Oct. 1962	31 May 1963	13
UNYOM	60 Days	11 June 1963	04 Sept. 1964	30
UNFICYP	30 Days	27 March 1964	27 March 1965	800
	90 Days	27 March 1965	Current	23,640*
UNIPOM	90 Days	22 Sept. 1965	24 March 1966	112
UNEFME	90 Days	27 Oct. 1973	24 July 1979	11,500*
UNDOF	90 Days	31 May 1974	Current	4,110*
UNIFIL	90 Days	19 March 1978	06 Oct. 1978	117
I.C.S.C.	90 Days	07 Aug. 1954	28 Jan. 1973	1,550
I.C.C.S.	90 Days	28 Jan. 1973	31 July 1973	352

* includes multiple tours; totals for current peace keeping service are correct to 31 March 1985

76. INTERNATIONAL COMMISSION FOR SUPERVISION AND CONTROL SERVICE MEDAL (INDO-CHINA) I.C.S.C.

Terms:

The medal is awarded for 90 days consecutive or non-consecutive service as a member of the Commission, calculated from the date the member came under the command of the Commission; or less than 90 days if such service is terminated by death, injury or any other disability received in carrying out official duties and a certificate is given to this effect by the Senior Military Advisor.

Obverse:

The emblem of the I.C.S.C. (crossed flags, left one with a maple leaf on it, right one with a central horizontal line, dove of peace where the flag staffs cross and lions between the flags facing left, centre and right). Around the edge are the words INTERNATIONAL COMMISSION FOR SUPERVISION AND CONTROL - PEACE. The word PEACE is located at the bottom and is larger and more widely spaced than the other words.

Reverse:

Map of Indochina showing the three countries, Vietnam, Cambodia, and Laos with their names written in the script of the countries.

Description:

Circular, 1.42 inches, bronze (a dark brown medal).

Mounting:

Floral attachment welded to top of medal joins a wide bar made up of three indented horizontal lines. The edges of the bar have vertical bars the same width as the horizontal bars and attached to these vertical bars is a narrow horizontal bar for the ribbon to pass through.

Ribbon:

1¼ inches; equal stripes left to right, Dark Green - White - Red. Green represents India and red represents Canada and Poland.

Naming:

Recipient's rank, surname and initials on the edge of the medal.

Dates:

Authorized 1967 for service after 7 August 1954 up to 28 January 1973

Issued:

1550 (31 March 1981) — 133 at any given time.

Example:

Lt. Col. William Bailey, C.D. — past Commanding Officer of the Seaforth Highlanders, Vancouver.

77.   INTERNATIONAL COMMISSION OF CONTROL AND SUPERVISION, VIETNAM 1973   I.C.C.S.

Terms:

This medal is awarded for 90 days service with the ICCS force between 28 January 1973 and 31 July 1973 (184 days in total).

Obverse:

The symbols of the four contributing countries are displayed in the centre with the Canadian Maple Leaf in the left upper position, Hungarian coat-of-arms, Polish Eagle and the Indonesian coat-of-arms. Around the edge are the words: INTERNATIONAL COMMISSION OF CONTROL AND SUPERVISION.

Reverse:

Laurel around the edge and the words in three lines: SERVICE / VIETNAM / 27 - 1 - 1973.

Description:

Circular, 1.42 inches, bright gold in colour (looks like it came out of a cracker jack box).

Ribbon:

1 1/2 inches; equal stripes: Red-White-Red-White - Green - White-Red-White-Red. (light green central stripe).

Naming:

Issued unnamed.

Dates:

28 January 1973 to 31 July 1973.

Issued:

352 (to Canadians)

Example:

Major Ian Duncan McLennan, O.M.M., C.D. - Senior Canadian Officer at the Cu Chi teamsite.

Note:

The medal issued to Canadians can be distinguished from those of the other three countries because it has a small maple leaf at the top of the laurel ring on the reverse side.

78. KING'S / QUEEN'S MEDAL FOR THE CHAMPION SHOT OF THE CANADIAN ARMY

Terms:

From 1923 to 1952, this medal was awarded to a member of the Canadian Army (Regular) who won the Best Shot competition at Bisley, Surrey or the Connaught Ranges. From 1953 to 1963, members of the RCMP were also eligible for the medal (none won it). Beginning in 1964, two medals were awarded, one to the Regular Army and one to the Militia and RCMP. After unification in 1968, one medal was awarded to the Regular Force

(Army, Air Force and Navy) and one to the Reserve Forces plus RCMP.

Bars:

Each medal is issued with a bar with the year of the award on it. Repeat winners add a bar to the original medal.

Obverse:

1. George V, uncrowned, facing left, in Field Marshall's uniform 1923.
2. George V, crowned, facing left, in robes. 1933 to 1936.
3. George VI, crowned, facing left, in robes. 1937 to 1952.
4. Elizabeth II, crowned bust, facing right. 1953 to present.

Reverse:

The figure of Fame rising from her throne, facing left, and placing a laurel wreath on a warrior with her right hand. The warrior, facing right, is standing on his right foot with his left raised and resting on the dias. He supports on his left knee a target having three arrows in the centre and in his right hand holds a bow and quiver full of arrows.

Description:

Circular, 1.42 inches, silver

Mounting:

Plain, straight non-swivelling suspender with a single toe claw.

Ribbon:

1 1/4 inches; watered, Crimson centre (9/16") with Black-White-Black edges, the black being twice as wide as the white.

Dates:

Instituted 1923 (not awarded 1940 to 1946 and not awarded in 1976)

Examples:

1923 — RSM Goodhouse
1924 — Cpl Livingstone
1925 — Lt. Burke
1926 — Cpl Livingstone
1927 — Lt. Burke
1928 — Maj Jeffery
1929 — Lt. Burke
1930 — Lt. Burke
1931 — Lt. Burke
1932 — Capt. Houlden
1933 — Lt. Coulter
1934 — Capt. Houlden
1935 — Sgt. Gregory
1936 — Cpl Robins
1937 — Lt. Molecey
1938 — Pte Wallace
1939 — Capt. Burke
1947 — Maj Burke
1948 — Lt. Fendick
1949 — OCdt Boa
1950 — OCdt Boa
1951 — OCdtBoa
1952 — LCol Johnson
1953 — Lt. McKeage
1954 — Capt Lawford
1955 — Lt. Warner
1956 — Sgt. Hardy
1957 — Lt. Derrick
1958 — SSgt White
1959 — Capt Barrett
1960 — WO2 Rowell
1961 — Pte Matthews
1962 — Lt. Lidgren
1963 — Sgt. Daigle
1964 — Capt. Molnar
1965 — Sgt. Bennett
1966 — Sgt. Daigle
1967 — Cpl. Fleming

CF (Regular)

1968 — Cpl Mercier
1969 — MWO White
1970 — Sgt Daigle
1971 — Cpl Hennick
1972 — Sgt WO Gibbery
1973 — Sgt L'Heureaux
1974 — Sgt Mercier
1975 — Sgt Mercier
1976 — nil *
1977 — Sgt Luscombe
1978 — Cpl McKay
1979 — Cpl Cromwell
1980 — Sgt McLellan
1981 — WO R. Surette
1982 — MCpl Daniel Demeuse
1983 — WO R. Surette
1984 — WO R. Surette

CF (Reserve) & RCMP

1963 — Sgt. T.A. Richardson
1964 — SSgt. C. Tremblay
1965 — Pte. Clerk
1966 — SSgt. Fish
1968 — Maj. Warner
1969 — Maj. Warner
1970 — Sgt Black RCMP
1971 — Maj. Warner
1972 — Maj. Warner
1973 — Lt. Kedziora
1974 — SSgt Black RCMP
1975 — WO Senetchko
1976 — Lt. Savinsky
1977 — Capt. Nicholson
1978 — Cpl. Oakie
1979 — Cpl. Oakie
1980 — Lt. Ferguson
1981 — Lt. Ferguson
1982 — Lt. M.R. Williams
1983 — Lt. M.R. Williams
1984 — Lt. K.E. Ferguson

* no award in 1976 as the Regular Force was commited to the Montreal Olympics.

Note:

In 1923, King George V approved the King's Medal for the Champion Shot of the Military Forces and granted one to Canada for Annual Competition by our military forces. From 1923 to 1962 (excluding 1940-1946), members of the Canadian Army (Regular), Canadian Army (Militia) and the RCMP competed annually for this medal. In 1963, the Queen (who's first Queen's Medal was presented in 1953), granted one additional Queen's Medal. One Queen's Medal was reserved for members of the Canadian Army (Regular) and one for the Canadian Army (Militia) plus the RCMP. Unification of the forces saw the terms, Canadian Forces (Regular) and Canadian Forces (Reserve)/RCMP as the two medals. The two Queen's Medals are awarded at the Canadian Forces National Small Arms Competitions, Connaught Ranges Ottawa, for the individual, Regular and Reserve (or RCMP), who has the highest aggregate score for rifle shooting in each stage of the Queen's Medal competition.

79. QUEEN'S MEDAL FOR THE CHAMPION SHOT OF THE ROYAL CANADIAN AIR FORCE

Terms:

The medal shall be competed for under small arms championship conditions during the Annual Prize Meeting of the Dominion of Canada Rifle Association and awarded to the winner of the competition with FN (C1A1) 7.62 mm Service Rifle. The competition includes: 1) 10 rounds at 600 yards; 2) 600 to 100 yards run, 2 shots at each 100 yards beginning at the 500 yard point; 3) 10 shots rapid firing at 300 yards; and, 4) Snap Shooting, 5 exposures, 2 shots each exposure. The member or the RCAF Regular Force or RCAF Reserves (Auxillary or Primary Reserve) with the best aggregate score will receive the Queen's Medal (Q.M.).

Bars:
Each medal is issued with a bar with the year of the award on it.

Obverse:
Elizabeth II, crowned head, facing right with the legend: ELIZABETH II DEI GRATIA REGINA F.D.

Reverse:
Hermes, mounted on a hawk in flight, holding a caduceus and about to throw a javelin. Inscription reads: THE QUEEN'S MEDAL FOR CHAMPION SHOTS OF THE AIR FORCES.

Description:
Circular, 1.42 inches, silver.

Mounting:

Plain, straight non-swivelling suspender with a single toe claw.

Ribbon:

1¼ inches; Crimson centre (⁹/₁₆″) with Dark Blue-Light Blue-Dark Blue edges, the Dark Blue approximately twice as wide as the Light Blue.

Dates:

Awarded from 1954 to 1967.

Examples:

1954 - FS JV Martin
1955 - F/L TW Gregory
1956 - Cpl S Goddard
1957 - LAC DA Green
1958 - LAC GE Sannachan
1959 - FS RH Cunnington
1960 - FS JW Brown
1961 - Cpl AF O'Brien
1962 - Cpl AF O'Brien
1963 - F/O OJ Ruckpaul
1964 - LAC CR Wesley
1965 - Cpl HR Peters
1966 - F/L OJ Ruckpaul
1967 - F/L MD Phoenix

CORONATION AND JUBILEE MEDALS

80. QUEEN VICTORIA'S DIAMOND JUBILEE MEDAL — 1897

Terms:
The medal was awarded to members of the Royal Family, Royal Household, Royal and distinguished guests attending the celebrations in June 1897 and to officers of the Army and Navy. It was also awarded to Senior Officers, Ministers and government officials who took part in the Jubilee ceremonies at which Her Majesty was present. The medals for the representative detachment of Canadian troops who had participated in the celebrations were personally presented to each man by H.R.H. The Prince of Wales at a ceremony held on the grounds of Buckingham Palace on 3 July 1897.

Bar:
There were no bars to this or any of the subsequent Coronation or Jubilee medals.

Obverse:
The crowned and veiled effigy of Queen Victoria, facing left with the inscription around the edge: VICTORIA D.G. REGINA ET IMPERATRIX F.D.

Reverse:
Inscription in 8 lines: IN / COMMEMORATION / OF THE / 60th YEAR OF THE / REIGN OF QUEEN / VICTORIA / 21 JUNE / 1897 within a wreath made up of roses, thistles and shamrocks tied at the base by a ribbon. At the top is a crown.

Description:
Circular, 1.25 inches, in silver and bronze (gold for Royal Family)

Mounting:
Ring attached to a small ring at the top of the medal.

Ribbon:
1 1/4 inches: Garter Blue with two Pale Blue stripes ($^3/_{16}$" wide) placed $^1/_{16}$" in from each edge.

Date:
21 June 1897

Total Issued:
338,796 (37 silver and 165 bronze were awarded to the Canadian Contingent on 3 July 1897—total to Canadians is unknown)

81.   KING EDWARD VII CORONATION MEDAL — 1902

Terms:

Awarded in a similar manner to Queen Victoria's Diamond Jubilee Medal. The Coronation was postponed from 26 June 1902 until 9 August 1902 due to the King's illness but the medal bears the original date.

Obverse:

Raised jugated busts of King Edward and Queen Alexandra, crowned and robed and facing left.

Reverse:

Royal Cypher ER VII in large script surmounted by a Crown with the date below 26 JUNE 1902.

Description:

Circular, 1.20 inches wide struck in silver and in bronze. The medal has a raised and ornamented rim in the form of a wreath of laurel banded by ribbon. It is surmounted by an Imperial Crown which goes outside the circle giving an oval appearance to the medal. Top of the Crown to bottom of the medal is 1.5 inches.

Mounting:

Ring attached $1/8$" below the top of the crown.

Ribbon:

$1 1/4$ inches; Dark Blue with narrow ($1/16$") White edges and a central Scarlet stripe ($1/4$" wide).

Dates:

26 June 1902.

Total Issued:

1 silver and 13 Bronze were awarded to the small Canadian contingent present for the Coronation. An additional 25 silver and 608 Bronze were received for distribution in Canada based on the number in the Canadian Contingent for the June Coronation date. These were distributed to approximately 1 officer and 30 other ranks in each military district. Other prominent Canadians probably also received the medal but the total is unknown.

Example:

Lt. Col. R.E.W.Turner, V.C. D.S.O. of the Q.O.C.H. commanded the small final Canadian contingent. (Turner later received KCB, KCMG).
Sir F.W. Borden, K.C.M.G.

82. KING GEORGE V CORONATION MEDAL — 1911

Terms:

Awarded as personal souvenirs of the coronation as per the previous two medals but with a wider distribution of the single silver type medal. The Canadian contingent to the Coronation received their medals on parade on 30 June 1911. Each Canadian Militia Unit was awarded 3 medals; one to the Commanding Officer; one to a Warrant Officer or N.C.O. and one to the oldest Private by service.

Obverse:

The conjoined busts of King George and Queen Mary, crowned and wearing the robes of state and facing left. They are encircled by a spray of roses on the left and a spray of laurel on the right entwined at the base with a ribbon. The designers initials B.M. are on the ribbon. (Sir Bertram Mackennel, M.V.O., R.A.)

Reverse:

Around the rim is a beaded circle and within is the Royal Cypher GRV surmounted by an Imperial Crown and below the date 22 JUNE 1911.

Description

Circular, 1.25 inches, silver.

Mounting:

Small ring attached to a smaller ring on the upper edge of the medal.

Ribbon:

1 1/4 inches; Garter Blue with two 1/8" central Red stripes.

Date:

22 June 1911

Total Issued:

15,901 with approximately 1000 to Canadians.

Example:

Colonel H.H. McLean who led the Canadian Contingent of 719 all ranks.

83. KING GEORGE V JUBILEE MEDAL — 1935

Terms:
Awarded to the Royal Family, Officers of State, officials and servants of the Royal Household, ministers, government officials, mayors, public servants, local government officials, members of the Navy, Army, Air Force and Police. Awarded in a like manner in Canada.

Obverse:
Conjoined busts of King George and Queen Mary crowned and robed, and facing left. Inscription
GEORGE V. AND QUEEN MARY MAY VI MCMXXV.

Reverse:
Royal Cypher GRI surmounted by the Royal Crown. On the left is the date in two lines MAY 6 / 1910 and on the right MAY 6 / 1935.

Description:
Circular, 1.25 inches, silver.

Mounting:
Ring attached to a claw at the top of the medal.

Ribbon:
1 1/4 inches; Red with 3 narrow stripes at each edge of Dark Blue-White-Dark Blue. The 3 stripes cover a 1/4" at each edge.

Dates:
6 May 1935.

Total Issued:
85,235 with 7,500 to Canadians. (1154 to the Canadian Forces)

Example:
Sergeant H.A. Larsen, R.C.M.P. (prior to his Polar Medal).

Terms:
Awarded as for the King George V Jubilee Medal.

Obverse:
Conjoined busts of King George VI and Queen Elizabeth, crowned and robed and facing left. No raised rim on the medal & no inscription.

Reverse:
Royal Cypher GRI surmounted by a large crown and below in two lines CROWNED / 12 May 1937. Around the rim of the medal is the inscription GEORGE VI QVEEN ELIZABETH (V in Queen rather than U)

Description:
Circular, 1.25 inches, silver.

Mounting:
Silver ring which passes through one claw at the top edge of the medal.

Ribbon:
1¼ inches; Garter Blue with 3 narrow stripes at each edge of White-Red-White. The 3 stripes cover a ¼ inch at each edge.

Dates:
12 May 1937

Total Issued:
90,279 with 10,089 to Canadians.

Example:
The Rt. Hon. Roland Michener, P.C., C.C., C.M.M., C.D., Q.C.

85.   QUEEN ELIZABETH II CORONATION — 1953

Terms:
Awarded as for the King George V Jubilee Medal as a personal souvenir to selected persons throughout the Commonwealth and Empire.

Obverse:
Queen Elizabeth Crowned and Robed facing Right. Remainder of the obverse is plain with no raised rim.

Reverse:
Royal Cypher E II R Surmounted by a large Crown. Inscription around the edge reads: QUEEN ELIZABETH II CROWNED 2nd JUNE 1953.

Description:
Circular, 1.25 inches, silver.

Mounting:
Silver ring which passes through a claw affixed to the top of the medal.

Ribbon:
1 1/4 inches; Dark red with 2 narrow (3/32") Dark Blue stripes in the centre (1/16" apart) and narrow (1/16") White stripes at each edge. Ladies awarded the medal can wear it on the left shoulder on their dress with the ribbon tied in the form of a bow.

Date:
2 June 1953 (medals awarded after the coronation)

Total Issued:
138,214 with 12,500 awarded to Canadians

Example:
W.O.1 F.E. Blatherwick, C.D. (RCAF)

86. QUEEN ELIZABETH II SILVER JUBILEE MEDAL — 1977

Terms:

In order that the list of those to be honored would be representative of all the regions of Canada, agencies of government at the federal, provincial and local levels were invited to propose the names of candidates for the Medal. National organizations in every important field of endeavor, including the professions, education and arts, veterans' groups, sports associations, philanthropic, charitable bodies and welfare services were also asked to participate by submitting nominations. All members of the Orders of Canada and Military Merit plus winners of Canadian Bravery Awards received the medal. Selection for the Armed Forces was based on merit with length of service and prestige of current appointment as secondary consideration.

Obverse:

Queen Elizabeth II wearing the high Imperial State Crown and facing right. The inscription around the rim reads: ELIZABETH II DEI GRATIA REGINA FID. DEF. The medal has a thin, smooth raised rim.

Reverse:

A large stylized maple leaf with C A N A D A around the top rim and along the lower rim 1952 E II R (small crown above the cypher) 1977. The designer's name HUNT is above 1977 (Dora DePedery-Hunt).

The reverse of the British medal has a St. Edward's crown at the top, a wreath of silver-birch foliage and catkins around the edge and the inscription in 6 lines: THE / 25TH YEAR OF / THE REIGN OF QUEEN / ELIZABETH II / 6 FEBRUARY / 1977.

Description:

Circular, 1.25 inches silver. (Canadian issue is slightly thicker than the British issue).

Mounting:

Silver Ring as per EIIR Coronation Medal.

Ribbon:

1¼ inches; Watered WHITE ribbon (representing silver) with narrow Cardinal-Red stripes at the outer edges. There is a narrow central stripe of Cardinal-Red with a Garter Blue stripe (⅛") on either side. Woman awarded medal with a bow as per Coronation Medal.

Date:

6 February 1977

Total Issued:

30,000 Canadians including 7000 to the Armed Forces (5500 Regular Forces and 1500 to the Reserve Forces). Breakdown for the Regular Forces was 1500 to officers (50% of Colonels; 25% Lt. Colonels; 20% Majors; 5% Captains & 5% Lieutenants) and 4000 to Other Ranks (50% CWOs; 25% MWOS; 15% WOs; 5% Master Corporals and 5% Corporals). The Reserve Force awards were made on a proportionate strength basis to the land, sea and air components, the Cadet Instructors List, the Canadian Rangers and to those holding Honorary Appointments. 30,000 Britains received the medal with 9,000 to the Armed Forces.

Examples:

Commander John Newbery, CD
Commander Ed Wallace, CD
Commander Gus Higuichi,CD
Commander David Johnson, CD
LCdr. Garth Olmstead, CD
Captain (N) Jack Thornton, OMM, CD
Captain (N) Stuart Alsgard, OMM, CD
CPO1 Ken Lloyd, CD
Mayor Muni Evers, City of New Westminster
Surgeon LCdr. Steve Hillier, CD
Commodore Wally Fox-Decent, CD

87.   CANADIAN CENTENNIAL MEDAL — 1967

Terms:
Awarded to selected people on the recommendation of governments and associations to commemorate the Centennial of the Confederation of Canada. The Armed Forces of Canada received almost 30% of the medals issued.

Obverse:
The Royal Cypher E II R surmounted by a Crown superimposed on a single Maple Leaf. Inscription around the circumference reads: CONFEDERATION CANADA CONFEDERATION.

Reverse:
The Coat of Arms of Canada with the dates 1867 - 1967 around the bottom rim of the medal.

Description:
Circular, 1.42 inches, silver. Medal has a thin plain raised rim.

Mounting:
A wide triangular ($^3/_{16}$" high) fixed suspender attached to the medal by a prominent single toe claw.

Ribbon:
1$^1/_4$ inches; White with four equally spaced narrow Red stripes and Red edges ($^3/_{16}$" wide) plus a single stitch of White thread on each edge.

Date:
1 July 1967

Total Issued:
29,500 of which 8500 were to the Armed Forces.

Examples:
W.O.1 F.E. Blatherwick, CD. (RCAF)
C.P.O.1 Loretta Barnett, HMCS Discovery
Lt. General William Carr, CMM, DFC, CD

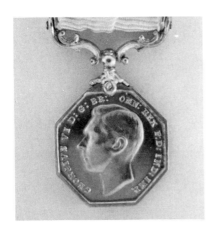 

Terms:

The medal is conferred on those who take an active part in an expedition which make notable advances in the exploration of the Polar Regions, and who undergo the hazards and rigours of these regions. The medal was awarded to members of the R.C.M.P. Ship St. Roche who patrolled extensively in the western Arctic in 1940-1942 and completed a west to east passage of the arctic in 1942. It was also awarded to the crew of the St. Roche who completed the east to west passage in 1944.

The medal was awarded to Major Andrew Taylor, RCE, on loan to the British Colonial Office, who commanded a base in Antarctic in 1944-46 as part of the Falkland Island and British Antarctic Survey.

Bars:

Each medal is awarded with a bar with the region and date on it.
ARCTIC 1940-42: (engraved) to the 8 R.C.M.P. crew members.
ARCTIC 1944: (embossed) to the 11 R.C.M.P. crew members.
ANTARCTIC 1944-45: to Major Taylor

Obverse:

George VI, uncrowned head facing left with the legend GEORGIVS VI D: G: BR: OMN: REX F: D: IND: IMP: (to the RCMP)

Elizabeth II, uncrowned head facing right with the legend

ELIZABETH II DEI:GRA:BRITT:OMN:REGINA:F:D: to Major Taylor

Reverse:

Sledging party of 6 in the foreground, with ice sledge with soil behind. Scott's HMS Discovery in middle distance in winter quarters. The volcanic Mount Erebus in the far distance.

Description:

Octagonal, 1.315 inches, silver.

Mounting:

Ornate scroll suspender.

Naming:
Rank and name engraved in capitals on the rim.

Ribbon:
1 1/4 inches; White (Silver rose emblem for a second bar)

Dates:
14 September 1904 to present.

Total Issued:
17 (3 with two bars) + 1 to a current Canadian + 1 Bronze medal

Examples:
Arctic 1940-42 & Arctic 1944 Bars
    S/Sgt. H.A. Larsen, FRGS
    Cst. G.W. Peters
    Cst. P.G. Hunt

Arctic 1940 - 42 Bar
    Cpl. M.R. Foster
    Cst. W.J. Parry
    Cst. A.J. Chartrand
    Cst. F.S. Farrar
    Cst. E.C. Hadley

Arctic 1944 Bar
    Cst. J.M. Diplock
    Spl Cst. R.T. Johnsen
    Spl. Cst. O. Andreasen
    Spl Cst. W.M. Cashin
    Spl. Cst. J.S. McKenzie
    Spl. Cst. R. Matthews
    Spl. Cst. G.B. Dickens
    Spl. Cst. L.G. Russell

Antarctic 1944 - 45 Bar
    Major. A. Taylor (an EIIR medal awarded due to long delay in the presentation)

Antarctic 1947
    Lt. Col. Dick Butson, G.C., O.M.M., O.St.J., C.D., M.B., F.R.C.P.(C) is a surgeon at McMaster University and a Reserve Medical Officer who won the ANTARCTIC 1947 medal while with a British expedition. Dr. Butson then moved to Canada. The medal is an EIIR medal due to the delay in its presentation. Dr. Butson was awarded the Albert Medal (gold) Land for rescuing a member of the expedition from a cravass and converted the Albert Medal to a George Cross in 1949. He is and will probably be the only member of the Order of Military Merit to also possess the George Cross.

Antarctic 1907 - 09 (Bronze Medal)
    Dr. W.A. Rupert Mitchell of Perth, Ont. (a surgeon on the Nimrod with Shackelton's expedition). King Edward VII in Admiral's uniform with legend EDWARDS VII REX IMPERATOR.

89.   CANADIAN FORCES DECORATION   C.D.

Terms:
Years: 12 Years Service
Service: Regular Force, Reserve Force & Officers of the Sea Cadets.
Ranks: All ranks (Officers, Warrant Officers, Men)
Dates: For anybody joining after 1 September 1939 - first awarded 1 September 1951; authorized 15 December 1949.
Superceded by: Current.
Bars: 10 additional years.

The Canadian Forces Decoration is awarded to officers and men of the Canadian Forces who, in an approved capacity, have completed a period of twelve (12) years service. The medal is awarded to all ranks who must have a good record of conduct during the last eight years of claimed service. The medal is awarded to the Regular Forces, Reserve Forces and to Officers of the Royal Canadian Sea Cadets. Service in the Regular and Reserve or Auxiliary Forces of the British Commonwealth of Nations shall count towards the medal if the last five years has been with the Canadian Forces and no other long service, good conduct or efficiency medal has been awarded for the same service. The medal may be awarded to persons in possession of any long service, good conduct or efficiency decoration or medal or clasps provided he has completed the full periods of qualifying service for each award and that no qualifying service towards one award is permitted to count towards the other. Service need not be continuous. This award supercedes all other awards for members joining the Canadian Forces after 1 Spetember 1939.

Bars:
A Bar shall be awarded for every subsequent period of ten (10) years qualifying service. The Bar is 1/4" high, has the Canadian Coat of Arms surmounted by a Crown in the centre and is made of tombac.

Obverse:
a) George VI, uncrowned coinage head, facing left.
b) Elizabeth II, uncrowned coinage head facing right. CANADA is at the bottom of the inscription around the rim.

Reverse:
A crown, three maple leaves and an eagle representative of the Navy, Army and Air Force from top to bottom. The word SERVICE is on a scroll at the base and a Fleur de Lis is on each side of the crown. The Royal Cypher of George VI is superimposed on the centre of his medal but is omitted for the Elizabeth II medal.

Description:
Decagonal (10 - sides representing the 10 provinces), $1^7/_{16}$ inches across the flats, raised busts. The George VI medal is 800 fine silver finished in silver gilt. The Elizabeth II medal is made of tombac (alloy of copper and zinc). Gilt in colour with the Elizabeth II medal brighter than the George VI medal.

Mounting:
a) George VI has a solid bar with CANADA on it and is attached to the medal by scroll arms welded to the top of the medal.
b) Elizabeth II does not have a bar and the ribbon passes through the scroll arms. A small maple leaf is at the base of the scroll arms.

Ribbon:
$1^1/_2$ inches; Gules with three central narrow Argent stripes (Orange-red with three central White stripes in common terms). A silver rosette is worn on the ribbon for each clasp awarded.

Dates:
Instituted 15 December 1949 and replaced all other awards for CF personnel joining after 1 September 1939. First awarded September, 1951.

Naming:
a) George VI — Name & rank engraved on reverse of CANADA tablet.
b) Elizabeth II — Name and rank stamped on edge.

Issued:
George VI — 13,500
Elizabeth II — 118,400 (to 1 January 1982; 2,400 per year approx.)
Bars: — 51,000 (to 1 January 1982)

Examples:
CWO F.E. Blatherwick, C.D. & bar — awarded C.D. September 1951
Cdr. F.J. Blatherwick, C.D. — awarded C.D. July 1976
Capt.(N) John Newbery, C.D. & bar — C.O., H.M.C.S. Discovery
Cdr. Bob McIlwaine, C.D. & bar — X.O., H.M.C.S. Discovery
LCdr. John Tyrrell, C.D. — H.M.C.S. Discovery

Note:
Beginning with the first Canadian Governor General, Rt. Honourable Vincent Massey, each Canadian Governor General has been awarded a C.D. on taking office. This is now a tradition and accounts for why Mr. Leger and Mr. Schreyer wear a C.D. (G.G. is ex-Officio, Commander in Chief of the Canadian Forces).

90. CANADIAN MEDAL FOR LONG SERVICE AND GOOD CONDUCT (MILITARY)

Terms:
Years: 18 years service
Service: Permanent Force Army (Permanent RCAF until August 1944)
Ranks: WOs, NCOs & Men
Dates: 23 Sept. 1932 (issued to those who joined prior to 01 Sept. 1939)
Superceded by: Canadian Forces Decoration CD
Bars: 18 additional years service (authorized August 1944)

Obverse:
i) Crowned bust of George V, in robes, facing left.
ii) Crowned head of George VI, facing left. (two types)
iii) Crowned bust of Elizabeth II, facing right: ELIZABETH II DEI GRATIA REGINA

Reverse:
Inscription in 4 lines, large letters:
FOR / LONG SERVICE / AND GOOD / CONDUCT

Description:
Circular, 1.42 inches, silver

Mounting:
Similar to George VI CD (with bar CANADA)

Engraving:
Around the edge, rank initials and surname

Ribbon:
1 1/4 inches, crimson with narrow white edges.

Totals:
George V — 700; George VI — 1,250; EIIR — 250; First Bars — 32 (1945-49); Second Bars — 2

Example:
B/Sgt. F.A. Price (E II R type)
S.M. (W.O.CL.1) J.E. TEASDALE R.C.E. (George V type)
PTE. D.J. Jones RCASC (George VI)

Note:
Officers with 12 years in the ranks could be awarded this medal.

91. COLONIAL PERMANENT FORCES LONG SERVICE & GOOD CONDUCT MEDAL

Terms:
Years: 18 years service
Service: Permanent Forces Army &
Air Force (Navy until 1925)
Ranks: Non-commissioned officers
and men
Dates: 1909 to 1932
Superceded by: Canadian Medal
for Long Service and Good Conduct

Obverse:
George V in Field Marshall's
uniform, facing left

Reverse:
Inscription in 4 lines, FOR / LONG SERVICE / AND GOOD / CONDUCT
and around the perimeter the words PERMANENT FORCES OF THE EM-
PIRE BEYOND THE SEAS.

Description:
Circular, 1.42 inches, silver.

Mounting:
Single toe claw with claw supports on the rim having inward scroll to a
plain, straight swivelling suspender.

Engraving:
Around the edge, number, rank, name and regiment.

Ribbon:
1909 to 1916: 1¼ inches, crimson with narrow central white stripe.
1916 to 1932: 1¼ inches, Dark Blue centre stripe (¹/₈"); narrow white stripe
on each side of the centre (³/₃₂") and wide crimson borders (⁷/₁₆")

Issued:
839 plus 1 to the RCAF

Example:
CONDR. (W.O.CL.1) W.J. Norris R.C.O.C.

92. LONG SERVICE AND GOOD CONDUCT (ARMY) MEDAL

Terms:
Years: 18 years service
Service: Permanent Forces of the Dominion of Canada
Ranks: Warrant Officers, Non-commissioned officers and men
Dates: 1902 to 1909
Superceded by: Colonial Permanent Forces LS & GC Medal

Obverse:
  i) Crowned & veiled bust of Queen Victoria facing left.
  ii) Edward VII in Field Marshall's Uniform facing left.

Reverse:
Inscription in four lines FOR / LONG SERVICE / AND / GOOD CONDUCT with the word CANADA above.

Description:
Circular, 1.42 inches, silver

Mounting:
Ornate scroll suspender, swivelling with double toe claw.

Engraving:
Rank, name, regiment.

Ribbon:
1 1/4 inches, crimson with 1/8 inch white centre stripe

Total Issued:
150 (mainly Edward VII)

93. ROYAL CANADIAN NAVY LONG SERVICE AND GOOD CONDUCT MEDAL

Terms:

Years: 15 Years Service

Service: Royal Canadian Navy - Permanent Force

Ranks: CPOs, POs, and Men (No Officers)

Dates: 19 June 1925 & issued to all those who joined prior to 01 September 1939 — Therefore awarded until Sept. 1954.

Superceded by: Canadian Forces Decoration (CD).

Bars: 15 additional years.

Obverse:

a) George V bust, Admiral's uniform, facing left.

b) George V coinage head facing left.

c) George VI, uncrowned coinage head, facing left (two types).

d) Elizabeth II, uncrowned coinage head, facing right (two types).

Reverse:

Starboard broadside view of a ship of the line at anchor, surrounded by a rope tied in a reef knot below. Legend reads: FOR LONG SERVICE AND GOOD CONDUCT around the edge.

Description:

Circular, 1.42 inches, silver.

Mounting:

Plain straight suspender with single toe claw.

Engraving:

Around the edge; rank, name, number and R.C.N.

Ribbon:

1¼ inches; Dark Blue with ¼" White edges.

Issued:

George V — 102

George VI & Elizabeth II: — approximately 200

Examples:

J.D. Pratt, CERA (bar to Medal March 1946)

J.R. Joslin, RPO (bar to Medal June 1946)

N.W. Crisp, C2MR3 (bar to Medal Aug. 1951)

Chief Stoker Thomas Herbert (21151); last George V issue 28/12/35.

94. ROYAL CANADIAN AIR FORCE LONG SERVICE AND GOOD CONDUCT MEDAL

Terms:

Years: 18 years service

Service: Royal Canadian Air Force - Permanent Air Force

Ranks: Warrant Officers, Non-Commissioned Officers and Men

Dates: 1 August 1944 approved for the RCAF - must be enrolled on or before 1 September 1939 - awarded until 1 September 1957.

Superceded by: Canadian Forces Decoration (CD).

Bars: 18 additional years; none awarded.

Obverse:

i) George VI, uncrowned coinage head, facing left.

ii) Elizabeth II, uncrowned coinage head, facing right.

Reverse:

Eagle in flight surmounted by Imperial Crown with the legend around the edge: FOR LONG SERVICE AND GOOD CONDUCT.

Description:

Circular, 1.42 inches, silver.

Mounting:

Ornate scroll suspender. The original RCAF Order stated that the "word CANADA shall be inscribed on the medal mount". Such a medal was never struck and the RCAF used the RAF medal.

Engraving:

Around the edge; rank, name, number

Ribbon:

1 1/4 inches; left half Dark Blue - right half Crimson with narrow White edges.

Issued:

Total: 487

Example:

W.O.2 N.J. McPhillips, R.C.A.F.

95. AIR EFFICIENCY AWARD

Terms:
Years: 10 years service
Service: RCAF (Auxiliary and RCAF Auxiliary Active Air Force
Ranks: All officers, Warrant Officers, NCOs, and Airmen
Dates: 17 August 1942 if service commenced prior to 1 September 1939.
Superceded by: Canadian Forces Decoration (CD)
Bars: 10 additional years; none awarded.

Obverse:
George VI, uncrowned coinage head, facing left

Reverse:
Inscription in 3 lines: AIR / EFFICIENCY / AWARD

Description:
Oval, 1 1/2 inches by 1 1/4 inches, silver.

Mounting:
Eagle with outspread wings; Canada used the RAF medal.

Engraving:
Rank & name on the edge.

Ribbon:
1 1/2 inches; Dark Green with two narrow central stripes of Pale Blue

Issued:
94

Examples:
W.O.1 Robert McDowall (later F/O)
G.C. J.M.W. St. Pierre, DFC, AFC
G.C. E.H.G. Moncrieff, OBE, AFC

Note:
There are no Elizabeth II Air Efficiency Awards to the RCAF (Auxiliary and Auxiliary Active Air Force) since any airman joining the reserves before 1 September 1939 would receive this medal by 1 September 1949 (10 years to receive award).

96.   CANADIAN EFFICIENCY DECORATION   E.D.

Terms:
Years: 20 years long and
meritorious service
Service: Non-permanent Active
Militia + Auxiliary and Reserve
RCAF
Ranks: Officers
Dates: 31 December 1931 for
members joining before 1 Sept.
1939.
Superceded by: Canadian Forces
Decoration CD

Obverse:
Oval oak wreath in silver tied with
gold enclosing the Royal Cypher and surmounted by the Crown in gold.
Cyphers: i) GRV ii) GRI iii) GVIR iv) EIIR

Reverse:
Naming engraved on the plain reverse.

Description:
Oval, 2¹/₈ inches by 1¹/₂ inches, silver. Bar with CANADA is worn at top of
the ribbon.

Mounting:
Small ring at top of oval through which ³/₄" yellow central stripe.

Ribbon:
1¹/₂ inches, green with ¹/₄" yellow central stripe.

Total Issued:
3,700 approximately.

Example:
BGen George Burnley Robertson, C.M.M., E.D.
Air Marshall Wilfred Austin Curtis, OC, CB, CBE, DSC, ED, CD.

Note:
War service counted double for the award of this decoration.

97. CANADIAN EFFICIENCY MEDAL

Terms:

12 years service; War Service counted double.

Service: Non-permanent Active Militia + RCAF (Auxiliary & Special Reserve)

Ranks: Warrant Officers, NCO's and men

Dates: 31 December 1931 for members joining before 1 Sept. 1939

Superceded by: Canadian Forces Decoration CD

Bars: 6 additional years for each bar

Obverse:

  i) George V: crowned bust, in robes, facing left.

  ii) George VI: crowned bust, in robes, facing left. (two types)

  iii) Elizabeth II: crowned bust, facing right. (two types)

Reverse:

Inscription in 3 lines: FOR / EFFICIENT / SERVICE.

Description:

Oval, 1½ inches by 1¼ inches, silver. Bars have Crown in center.

Mounting:

Two large laurel leaves attached to a horizontal bar with a scroll superimposed with the word CANADA on it.

Ribbon:

1¼ inches, green with ⅛ inch yellow border stripes.

Total Issued:

George V	1,600	1st Bar	3,200	3rd (1945 +)	140
George VI	10,600	2nd bar	845	4th Bars (1949 +)	18
Elizabeth II	450			5th Bars (1957 +)	3

Examples:

C.S.M. (W.O. CL. 2) E.G. Payne Q.O.R. of C. with 3 bars (George V type)

Sgt. J.R. ,MacKinnon R.C.A. (George VI type)

Pte. J.E.C. Avery (EIIR type shown in photo)

98. COLONIAL AUXILIARY FORCES OFFICERS' DECORATION

V.D.

Terms:
Years: 20 years service
Service: Militia
Ranks: Officers
Dates: 1901 to 31 December 1931
Superceded by: Canadian Efficiency Decoration ED

Obverse:
Oval band with the Imperial Cypher (VRI, ERI VII, GRI) in silver gilt in the center surrounded by a chased band of silver inscribed COLONIAL AUXILIARY FORCES. The badge is surmounted by the Imperial Crown in silver gilt.

Reverse:
Plain except rank, name & unit in the crown area at top.

Description:
Oval, 1 1/2 inches by 1 7/16 inches, silver and silver gilt.

Mounting:
Small ring behind top of the crown attaches to small ring attached to bottom of thin wire suspender. The top broach is decorated with laurel and is silver.

Total Issued
VRI — 850
ERI VII — 250
GRV — 1,600

Ribbon:
1 1/4 inches, dark green.

Examples:
Capt & Bt.Maj. E.R. Hale, V.D., — C.A.S.C.
MGen. W.W. Foster, C.M.G., D.S.O., V.D.

Terms:

Years: 20 years service (war service counted double).

Service: Non-permanent Active Militia (including RNCVR & RCAF Aux.)

Ranks: Warrant Officers, NCO's and Men

Dates: 4 February 1901 to 23 September 1931.

Superceded by: Canadian Efficiency Medal

Bars: Nil

Obverse:

a) Queen Victoria, diademed & veiled bust, facing left.

b) Edward VII, bust in Field Marshall's uniform, facing left.

c) George V, in Field Marshall's uniform, facing left.

Reverse:

Ornamental shield bearing legend in 5 lines: FOR / LONG SERVICE / IN THE / COLONIAL AUXILIARY / FORCES. Above the shield is an Imperial Crown with a spray of oak leaves to the left and a spray of laurel on the right.

Description:

Circular, 1.42 inches, silver.

Mounting:

Plain, straight suspender with single toe claw plus claw supports on the rim having an inward scroll.

Ribbon:

1 1/4 inches; Dark Green

Issued:

Victoria - 1,350; E.R.I. VII - 750; G.R.V. - 4,300 There are probably more that are not on the official rolls.

Example:

C.S.M. W.S. Montgomery - Q.O.R. of C.

100. MERITORIOUS SERVICE MEDAL M.S.M.

Terms:
Years: 21 years service - awarded after discharge.
Service: Permanent Forces
Ranks: Warrant Officers, Staff Sergeants & Sergeants (Senior NCOs).
Dates: 1902 until 1958 (must be enrolled prior to 1 Sept. 1939).
Superceded by: nil (those entitled to just the C.D. not eligible for M.S.M.)
Bars: For additional acts of gallantry.

For Service:
Awarded to Warrant Officers and Senior NCOs who were discharged with 21 years service (18 if disabled), who had earned the Long Service and Good Conduct Medal and was limited to 40 in wear at any one time (increased to 75 in 1928 & 100 in 1939).

For Gallantry:
In 1916, the MSM was awarded to all ranks "who are duly recommended for the grant in respect of gallant conduct in the performance of military duty otherwise than in action against the enemy, or in saving, or attempting to save the life of an officer or soldier, or for devotion to duty in a theatre of war". It was cancelled for gallantry 7 September 1928 and replaced by the British Empire Medal.

Obverse:
a) Edward VII, in Field Marshall's uniform, facing left.
b) George V, in Field Marshall's uniform, facing left.
c) George V. coinage head, facing left.
d) George VI, uncrowned coinage head, facing left. (two types)
e) Elizabeth II, uncrowned coinage head, facing right. (two types)

Reverse:
Inscription in 3 lines: FOR / MERITORIOUS / SERVICE within two laurel leaves broken at the top by an Imperial Crown. A horizontal line is above the bow of the laurel. Edward VII & George V medals have CANADA above the crown.

Description:
Circular, 1.42 inches, silver

Mounting:
Ornated Scroll Suspender with double toe claw.

Ribbon:

1902 - 1916: 1¼ inches, Crimson (changed as confused with V.C. ribbon).

1916 - 1917: 1¼ inches, Crimson with White edges (⅛").

1917 - on: 1¼ inches, Crimson with White edges (⅛") and narrow White central stripe.

Issued:

Gallantry: 1427 - George V

2 - George V in Admiral's uniform (Navy)

1 - George V Air Force with Blue-Crimson-White edges & White central stripe ribbon.

Service:

50 — Edward VII

60 — George V (Field Marshall's uniform)

25 — George V (Crowned bust)

100 — George VI (two types)

40 — Elizabeth II (two types)

Example:

C.S.M. W.M. Salter, No. 12 Coy, Canadian Forestry Corps.

101 ROYAL CANADIAN NAVY VOLUNTEER OFFICER'S DECORATION V.D.

Terms:
Years: 20 years service
Service: RCNVR (and to the RCN
(R) after 1 Jan. 1946
Ranks: Officers
Dates: 1938 for members joining
before 1 September 1939
Superceded by: Canadian Forces
Decoration CD

Obverse:
Oval medallion in silver gilt formed
by the GRI Cypher surrounded by
a loop of cable tied at the bottom in
a reef knot and surmounted by a
gilt Crown.

Reverse:
Naming only.

Description:
Oval, silver

Mounting:
Small ring at top of the crown through which a large ring passes. Ribbon attached to large ring.

Ribbon:
1 1/2 inches. dark green centre, flanked by thin red stripes with wide navy blue borders.

Total Issued:
47

Examples:
Commodore R.I. Hendy, VD
Surgeon Captain John Duckworth, VD
Commander (later Captain) A.W. Ross, OMM, VD (awarded OMM 13/06/73)

102. ROYAL CANADIAN NAVY VOLUNTEER RESERVE LONG SERVICE AND GOOD CONDUCT MEDAL

Terms:

Years: 12 years service (with maximum number of good conduct badges)

Service: R.C.N.V.R. (and RCN (R) after 1 Jan. 1946.

Ranks: Men only (no Officers)

Dates: 1938 to 1 Jan. 1946; then awarded to unified RCN (R) for men who joined before 1 September 1939.

Superceded by: Canadian Forces Decoration CD

Bars: 12 years additional service

Obverse:

George VI, uncrowned coinage head, facing left

Reverse:

A starboard, broadside view of the battleship DREADNOUGHT. Legend curved at the bottom reads DIUTURNE FIDELAS. (For Long and faithful service).

Description:

Circular, 1.42 inches, silver.

Mounting:

Plain straight suspender with single toe claw.

Ribbon:

1½ inches. Wide dark green centre, medium red stripes on each flank and wide navy blue borders.

Total Issued:

200 approximately

Note:

No Elizabeth II medals to RCNVR & RCN (R) as anybody enlisting before 1 September 1939 would receive this medal by 1 September 1951 (12 years to qualify). This applies to RCN (R) LS & GC Medal as well.

103. ROYAL CANADIAN NAVAL RESERVE OFFICER'S DECORATION

R.D.

Terms:
Years: 15 years service (with prescribed training periods)
Service: RCN (R)
Ranks: Officers
Dates: 23 April 1937 to 1 January 1946.
Superceded by: RCNVR-VD

Description:
Same as for RCNVR-VD described previous page.

Ribbon:
1 1/2 inches, dark green to 1941; then green with white edges

Total Issued:
37

104. ROYAL CANADIAN NAVAL RESERVE LONG SERVICE AND GOOD CONDUCT MEDAL

Terms:
Years: 15 years service (of very good assessments)
Service: RCN (R)
Ranks: Men (no Officers)
Dates: 1938 to 1 January 1946
Superceded by: RCNVR Long Service and Good Conduct Medal

Description:
Same as for RCNVR LS & GC

Ribbon:
1 1/4 inches, green until 1941; then green with white edges and central white stripe, each white stripe 3/16"

Total Issued:
55 plus 1 clasp

105. THE SERVICE MEDAL OF THE ORDER OF ST. JOHN

Terms:

Awarded in Canada for 12 years service to the St. John Ambulance organization (15 years in Great Britain).

Bars:

Awarded for 5 additional years. Bars are slip on type, silver, laureled with a St. John Cross in the centre.

Obverse:

The bust of Queen Victoria, crowned and veiled, facing right, with a ring around the outside with the legend: VICTORIA + D + G + BRITT + REG + F + D + IND + IMP.

Reverse:

The Royal Arms within the Garter bearing the legend HONI · SOIT · QUI · MAL · Y · PENSE · Above this is a Crown and below it the Prince of Wales' Feathers. On each side is the Badge of the Order each bearing a shield, the one on the left charged with the Arms of the Order and that on the right with the Arms of the Prince of Wales. The whole device rests upon a sprig of St. John's Wort. This central motif is surrounded by a border bearing the words: · MAGNUS · PRIORATUS · HOSPITALS · SANCTI · JOHANNIS · JERUSALEM · IN · ANGLIA.

Description:

Circular, 1 1/2 inches, silver (made in cupro nickel, rhodium plated).

Mounting:

Single toe claw with inwards scrolls going to a straight bar.

Ribbon:

1 1/2 inches; Black-White-Black-White-Black in equal stripes. A single stitch of White is at each edge. Miniature metal crosses are worn in undress for each bar up to three. At four bars, one rolled gold cross is worn.

Naming:

Currently issued unnamed; formerly on the rim.

Dates:

1898 - Current.

106. ROYAL CANADIAN MOUNTED POLICE LONG SERVICE MEDAL

Terms:
Awarded for 20 years service with good and satisfactory conduct.

Bars:
25 years - bronze bar with one star; 30 years - silver bar with 2 stars; 35 years - 18k gold bar with three stars.

Obverse:
1) GeorgeV:
   crowned bust in robes, facing left, inscription GEORGIVS • V • D • G • BRITT • OMN • REX • ET • INDIAE • IMP •
2) George VI:
   uncrowned, coinage head, facing left, inscription GEORGIVS VI D : G : BR : OMN : REX ET IN-DIAE IMP :
3) George VI:
   uncrowned, coinage head, facing left, inscription GEORGIVS VI DEI GRATIA REX (introduced in 1948)
4) Elizabeth II:
   uncrowned, coinage head, facing right, inscription ELIZABETH II DEI GRATIA REGINA

Reverse:
RCMP badge with the words FOR LONG SERVICE / AND GOOD CON-DUCT around the edge. There is also a French version.

Description:
Circular, 1.42 inches, silver (800 fine at present)

Mounting:
Claw at top of medal to a straight bar.

Ribbon:
1 1/4 inches; Blue with 2 Yellow stripes, 1/8" wide & 1/4" from the edge.

Naming:
Rank and name on rim.

Dates:
1933 - Current

Total issued:

George V	388	George VI (second type)	329
George VI (first type)	384	Elizabeth II	4000 plus

Examples:

J.E.R. Rochon (EIIR type)

Inspector Henry Larsen (George VI-second type); his medals are on display at the St. Roche Ship in Vancouver and include the 39-45 Star, Atlantic Star, Pacific Star, 39-45 War Medal, two Bar Polar Medal, George V Jubilee Medal, RCMP LS with Silver Bar (note: RCMP did not receive the C.V.S.M.)

107. KING'S POLICE AND FIRE SERVICES MEDAL

Terms:

Awarded to members of a recognized police force or regularly organized fire service who have performed acts of exceptional courage and skills or have exhibited conspicuous devotion to duty.

Obverse:

Crowned bust of George V or George VI, in robes facing left.

Reverse:

An erect armed figure robed and helmeted with a large sword in his right hand, and a shield in his left inscribed TO GUARD MY PEOPLE. A lighted lantern sits at his right foot and in the middle background is a fortified city. In exergue are the words, FOR GALLANTRY.

Description:

Circular, 1.42 inches, silver.

Naming:

On the rim.

Mounting:

Silver ring as per the George Medal.

Ribbon:

1³/₈ inches; Dark Blue, Silver stripes at edge and in the centre, thin Red stripe in the middle of each of the Silver stripes.

Dates:

1909 to 1952 when superceded by the George Medal

Total Issued:

15-George V; 47-George VI (to 1950 there were 8 to RCMP, 10 Firemen).

Examples:

Sgt. Major T.B. Caulkin, RCMP - for Distinguished Service

Inspr. Robson Armitage, RCMP - 8 March 1939 for gallantry during a shootout.

Cpl. Hugh Russell, RCMP, 1947 - for going down a gas filled well to rescue 2 men.

Capt. Elgin R. Jones, Orillia Fire Department — George VI issue.

108   POLICE EXEMPLARY SERVICE MEDAL

Terms:

A person is eligible to be awarded the medal if the person:

a) was a serving officer on 1 August 1980 or after that date;

b) has completed a minimum of twenty years of full-time service with one or more recognized Canadian police forces, including full-time police-cadet training, of such good standard as to warrant an award. The period of service, in whole or in part, must not have been recognized by any other official, national long service, good conduct or efficiency decoration or medal;

c) the person is nominated by the chief or the director of the police force in which the nominee has served or by the chairman of the authority in charge of the police force and that person must state that during the period of service, no serious disciplinary action has been taken or is pending in respect of the nominee and that the conduct and performance or the nominee has been judged as being exemplary;

d) members of the Royal Canadian Mounted Police and the Canadian Forces Military Police are not eligible but time in these organizations may count towards this medal for former members of the RCMP and CF Military Police where such time was not counted towards the RCMP Long Service and Good Conduct Medal or the Canadian Forces Decoration.

Bars:

For each additional ten years of exemplary service. The bar is a plain silver bar with a stylized maple leaf in the centre.

Obverse:

The stylized maple leaf in the centre bears the scales of justice with the words EXEMPLARY SERVICE — SERVICES DISTINGUES circumscribed on the outside circle.

Reverse:

The Royal Cypher E II R surmounted by a crown in the centre.

Description

A circular, silver medal, 36 mm in diameter. The Maple Leaf fits inside the circle and is attached to the circle at ten points such that there are openings in the medal.

Mounting:

A Fleur de Lis claw attached to the top of the medal which becomes a wide silver bar through which the ribbon attaches.

Naming:

Name is engraved around the edge.

Ribbon:

1 1/4 inches; equal stripes Blue-Gold-Blue-Gold-Blue (identical to the ribbon for the former unofficial Chiefs of Police Service Medal); a small silver maple leaf is worn on the ribbon in undress to signify a bar.

Dates:

Letters Patent signed by the Queen 12 August 1983 and award of the medal is available to all police officers who were serving on or after 1 August 1980. (the 1 August 1980 date was chosen as that was the date that former Prime Minister Trudeau told the Conference of Chiefs of Police that an official medal would be awarded to Police Officers by the Canadian Government). First awards appeared in the Canada Gazette, Part 1, 15 October 1983.

Issued:

1983: 663 medals; 194 first bars; 19 second bars
1984: 5553 medals; 1554 first bars; 24 second bars

Examples:

Deputy Chief Ed Cadenhead, New Westminster Police , Medal & Bar March 1984
Chief Ken Brown, New Westminster Police, Medal, March 1984
A.J. Bell of Mont-Joli, Quebec medal and two bars gazetted, Oct. 1983
T. Sims of Meaford, Ontario medal and two bars gazetted, Oct. 1983
N.L. Sterritt of Brockville, Ontario medal and two bars gazetted, Oct. 1983
R.W. Warden of Guelph, Ontario medal and two bars gazetted, Oct. 1983

Note:

This medal replaces the Canadian Association of Chiefs of Police Service Medal. The same ribbon was chosen for this official award as the unofficial award as the ribbon is well known amongst policemen. Since the Chiefs of Police Medal was an unofficial award, the two medals should not be worn together. This medal follows the RCMP Long Service Medal in order of sequence.

Terms:

This medal may be awarded to a Canadian who is an employee of a Canadian correctional service on or after 11 June 1984 and has completed a minimum of twenty years of full-time paid service, not necessarily continuous, with one or more correctional services in Canada, of such good standard as to warrant an award, ten years of which must be as a peace officer in an institution, parole office or pro-

bation office. No period of service, in whole or in part, that has been recognized by any other long service, good conduct or efficiency decoration or medal awarded by the Crown in Right of Canada shall count as service for award of the Medal. Full-time unrecognized service in the Canadian Forces as a Military Policeman, in a recognized Police Force in Canada or in any other occupation eligible for award of a medal for exemplary service may count as qualifying service.

Bars:

A person who has been awarded the Medal is eligible to be awarded a Bar in respect of each additional TEN year period of full-time service with one or more correctional services in Canada, if that service is of such good standard as to warrant an award. The Bar to the Medal is a plain bar with a stylized maple leaf centred.

Obverse:

A stylized maple leaf bearing a key and torch, crossed, circumscribed with the words: EXEMPLARY SERVICE • SERVICES DISTINGUES.

Reverse:

The Royal Cypher centred.

Description:

A circular, silver medal, 36 mm in diameter. The Maple Leaf fits inside the circle and is attached to the circle at ten points such that there are openings in the medal between the maple leaf and the circle.

Mounting:

A Fleur de Lis claw attached to the top of the medal which becomes a wide silver bar through which the ribbon is attached.

Naming:

Name is engraved around the edge.

Ribbon:

1 1/4 inches; five equal stripes: Green-Gold-Green-Gold-Green. A small silver maple leaf is worn on the ribbon in undress to signify a bar.

Dates:
Letters Patent signed 11 June 1984 by Queen Elizabeth.
Issued:

Examples:

Notes:
This medal follows the Police Exemplary Service Medal in precedence.

110.   THE MERITORIOUS SERVICE CROSS   M.S.C.

Terms:
A member of the Canadian Forces or a person who holds an honorary appointment made in accordance with Article 3.06 of the Queen's Regulations and Orders for the Canadian Forces may be awarded the Meritorious Service Cross. Award of the Cross is open to all ranks for the performance of a military deed or a military activity in an outstandingly professional manner of such a rare high standard that it  brings considerable benefit to, or reflects great credit on, the Canadian Forces, where such deed or activity is completed after the coming into force of these Regulations. The M.S.C. may be awarded posthumously.

Bars:
A second award of the Cross for the terms as set out above shall be recognized by the awarding of a bar. The bar is a plain silver bar having a maple leaf in the centre.

Obverse:
A cross with a maple leaf within a circle in the centre and laurel wreath between the arms of the cross. A Royal Crown on the upper arm forms part of the mounting.

Reverse:
The Royal Cypher (E II R) with a crown on top and within a double circle the words: MERITORIOUS SERVICE MERITOIRE; small maple leaf at the bottom of the double circle separates the words, Meritorious and Meritoire.

Description:
A Greek Cross of Silver, ends splayed and convexed, ensigned with the Royal Crown. The Cross is 1½ inches across and between the arms of the Cross is laurel wreath.

Mounting:
The Royal Crown attaches to the top of the upper arm of the Cross and is attached to the wide silver bar through which the ribbon passes by the tip of the Crown.

Naming:
The name of the recipient is engraved on the medal.

Ribbon
1¼ inches (32 mm); Bright Blue ribbon with two white stripes (¼" or 6 mm) positioned ⅛" (4 mm) from each edge.

Dates:
Approved by Queen Elizabeth 16 June 1984.

Issued:
Nil to March 1985

Examples:
Nil

111   SPECIAL SERVICE MEDAL

Terms:
This medal is to be awarded (as determined by the Governor in Council) to members of the Canadian Forces for service performed under exceptional circumstances in a clearly defined locality for a specified duration, not necessarily in a theatre of active operation. The medal may also be awarded to persons who are not members of the Canadian Forces. (The Medal will be awarded in a manner similar to the British General Service Medal).

Bars:
The medal will only be issued with a bar representing the particular special service. Where a member serves in a locality to warrant the award of a second medal, a bar only will be added to the original medal.

Obverse:

A Maple Leaf surrounded by a laurel wreath.

Reverse:

In the centre the Royal Cypher (E II R) with the Royal Crown above and around the edge: SPECIAL SERVICE SPECIAL (the word Service at the bottom).

Description:

A circular, cupro nickel, 1.42 inches (36 mm) medal.

Mounting:

A single toe claw attaches to the top of the medal and to the centre of a straight bar. The Clasps are attached to this bar.

Naming:

Engraved on the edge of the medal.

Ribbon: 1 1/4 inches, Dark Green Centre (1/2"), flanked with White (3/16") and edged with Red (3/16").

Dates:

Approved by Queen Elizabeth 16 June 1984.

Issued:

Nil to March 1985

Examples:

Nil — first medal could possibly be awarded to members of the Canadian Forces serving in the Middle East.

Note:

This medal will come immediately after the Canadian Korean War Medal and before the United Nations Service Medal for Korea. While this would appear to be an anomoly breaking up this U.N. pair, it is done as this medal is considered to be in the class of war medals and the last Canadian War Medal was the Korean War Medal. The U.N. medals are peace keeping medals. In practice, it will be highly unlikely that serving members will have this happen.

112. CANADIAN MEMORIAL CROSS

Terms:

A Memorial Cross will be issued as a memento of personal loss and sacrifice on the part of mothers and widows of personnel of the Royal Canadian Navy, The Canadian Army, or the Royal Canadian Air force (now the Canadian Forces) who have laid down their lives for their country whilst in, or proceeding to or returning from an area of hostilities outside of Canada or who die of causes attributable to service in such areas, in consequence of any action undertaken by Canada under the United Nations charter, the North Atlantic Treaty, or any other instrument for collective defence that may be entered into by Canada (Order in Council PC 5812, 5 December 1950). The Order in Council is applicable to all current members of the Canadian Forces by virtue of the Canadian Forces Reorganization Act.

World War I (Order in Council PC 2374, 1 December 1919)

A Cross or Crosses may be issued in respect of each sailor or soldier who:
a) was killed in action during World War I;
b) died while on active service during World War I; or
c) died or dies from causes attributable to service during World War I in the naval or military forces, whether his death occurred or occurs while serving on active service or subsequent thereto except that a cross may only be issued to the widow or her next of kin if she was married to the sailor or soldier at the time of his discharge.

The order states that if a soldier or sailor is survived by both a widow and a mother, two Crosses may be issued, one to the widow and one to the mother. If a mother to whom a Cross might have been awarded has died or dies before a Cross is issued, the Cross may be issued to the person designated by the Minister to be the eldest surviving next of kin of the mother, and if a widow to whom a Cross might have been awarded has died or dies before a Cross is issued, the Cross may be delivered to the person designated by the Minister to be the eldest surviving next of kin of the widow. The Cross may be awarded to the mother or widow of a sailor or soldier of Canada or Newfoundland.

Sailor means any person who served during World War I in:
a) Any branch of the Royal Canadian Naval Service;
b) any other of the Naval Forces of His Majesty; or
c) the naval forces of one of the countries allied with His Majesty during World War I, if, for (b) or (c) that person was born or domiciled in Canada or Newfoundland or was an ordinary resident in Canada or Newfoundland at any time during the period between 3 August, 1904, and the date on which he commenced to so serve.

Soldier means any person who served during World War I in:
a) the Canadian Expeditionary Force; or
b) any of the other military forces of His Majesty; or
c) the military forces of one of the countries allied with His Majesty during World War I with the same provisions for (b) and (c) as for a sailor.

World War II (Order in Council PC 4210, 27 August 1940)
Similar to World War I Order but includes the term Airman.

Post World War II (Order in Council PC 1976-1715, 4 November 1976)
Amalgamated all previous O.I.C.s relating to the Memorial Cross and added:

Merchant Seaman which means any person who served during World War II as Master, Officer, or crew of a ship registered in Canada, a United Kingdom ship or a registered ship of one of the countries allied with His Majesty during World War II.

Fire Fighter which means a person who served during World War II as a member of the Corps of (Civilian) Canadian Fire Fighters for Service in the United Kingdom.

Obverse:
Royal Cypher G R I or G VI R or E II R in the centre. An Imperial Crown at the end of the upper arm and a maple leaf on the end of the two side arms and the lower arm.

Reverse:
Engraved with the number, rank and name of the officer or man commemorated. Also has a silver identification mark on the lower arm.

Description:
The cross is a cross patonce in silver surmounted on a wreath of laurel. In the upper arm is an Imperial Crown, and on the two side arms and the lower arm a Maple Leaf. A smaller St. George Cross is superimposed on the larger with the Royal Cypher in the centre in raised letters. The cross, a $^3/_4$ scale model of the Military Cross is 32 mm by 32 mm and has a dull or matte finish sterling silver .925 fine.

Mounting:
There is a small rigid ring on top of the upper arm through which a small loose ring fits. Prior to 1945, the cross was worn around the neck with the ribbon passing through the loose ring. After January, 1945, the loose ring was attached to a fixed ring on the bottom of a brooch. This brooch is 32 mm wide and has the form of the two side arms of the cross.

Naming:
Number, rank and name of the officer or man commemorated is engraved on the back of the cross.

Ribbon:
Purple, rayon ribbon, 10 mm wide and 750 mm long for those issued prior to January 1945 to be worn around the neck. After January 1945, no ribbon.

Date:
23 March 1919 the Cross was announced in the House of Commons of Canada.

118

Issued:

WWI, 60,000 plus; WWII, 60,000 plus (5,000 of which had G R I Royal Cypher and 4 were to civilian firefighters); Korea, 1,000 plus (516 Canadians killed in Korea); post Korea, unknown.

Examples:

WWI   Capt. Francis Quigley, DSO, MC & Bar (RFC) died 18 October, 1918
        Flt. Cdr. A.J. Chadwick, DSC, (RNAS) died 28 July, 1917
        Lt. Samuel Lewis Honey, VC, DCM, MM, 78th Cdn. Infantry, died 30 September 1918

WWII   S/L Henry W. McLeod, DSO, DFC & Bar (443 Sqd. RCAF) died 27 September, 1944
        T/Lt. Robert Hampton Gray, VC, DSC, (RCNVR) died 19 August, 1945
        Lt. Col. R.M. Crowe, Commanding Officer, P.P.C.L.I., died 24 July, 1943

Korea   Sgt. R.H. Richards, P.P.C.L.I., died 27 September, 1952

Peace   F/L P. Wilcox (408 Squadron) died 12 October, 1967

113. FIREFIGHTER EXEMPLARY SERVICE MEDAL

Terms:

This medal has just been announced, being approved Aug. 29, 1985. The actual wording for the terms has not yet been released. We understand as of the date of this publication that it will apply to either full time or volunteer firemen with 20 years exemplary service. A bar is to be awarded for each additional 10 years of exemplary service.

Description:

The same as the POLICE EXEMPLARY SERVICE MEDAL except for a destinctive centre symbol of crossed fire axes with a Maltese cross bearing a superimposed fire hydrant.

Reverse:

Identical to POLICE EXEMPLARY SERVICE MEDAL.

Physical Description:

Identical to POLICE EXEMPLARY SERVICE MEDAL.

Mounting:

Identical to POLICE EXEMPLARY SERVICE MEDAL.

Ribbon:
1 1/4 inches; 5 equal stripes; 3 red, 2 gold.
Issued:
Nil to September 1985.

114.   COAST GUARD EXEMPLARY SERVICE MEDAL

Terms:
This medal is still in the planning stage in August 1985. It will be for twenty years exemplary service.

Description:
As for the POLICE EXEMPLARY SERVICE MEDAL except for a distinctive centre symbol.

No Picture Available

Ribbon:
1 1/4 inches. Will have gold as two of the stripes.

Dates:
to be announced.

MENTIONS IN DESPATCHES (M.I.D.)

Terms:

Originally a mechanism to notify higher authorities of deserving officers' services in the field or at sea, the practice of Mentions in Despatches was extended to all ranks in the mid-1840s. Most of the M.I.D.s are merely lists of names but sometimes (particularly in the Navy), specific deeds are documented. Publication of the person's name in the London Gazette and later the Canadian Gazette is needed for an M.I.D. to be official.

Description:

World War I — A bronze, multiple-leaved emblem ($1\frac{3}{8}$" x $\frac{3}{8}$" when worn on the medal and 1" x $\frac{1}{4}$" when worn on the ribbon in undress). Secured to the ribbon by bent over pins although some had holes for sewing on. Worn on the Victory Medal.

World War II — A single bronze oak leaf, $\frac{3}{4}$" long and $\frac{5}{16}$" wide (same
& Korea   size for medal or ribbon in undress). Secured by bent over pins but some had holes for sewing onto the ribbon. Worn on the 1939-45 War Medal or the Canadian Korea Medal.

Issued:

WWI — 5,467
WWII — RCAF - 2,197, RCN - 1,037, Army - 6,432
Korea — RCAF - 0, RCN - 33, Army - 246

Examples:

Canada Gazette 13 June 1953, Page 1713: Her Majesty the QUEEN has been graciously pleased to approve the award of a Mention-in-Despatches to the following personnel serving in HMC ships, for service in Korean waters: Captain W.M. Landymore, CD, RCN HMCS Iroquois. "Captain Landymore, during $5\frac{1}{2}$ months in command of Iroquois in the Korean War area, has led his ship many times in displaying much resource and devotion to duty. The spirit and cheerfulness of his ship's company when damaged in action were very commendable.

KING'S/QUEEN'S COMMENDATION FOR BRAVE CONDUCT

Terms:

In World War I, some civilians were commended for 'good service' but it was not until World War II that commendations for civilians were made on a regular basis and became like a civilian 'Mention-in-Despatches'. The award is made for gallantry where the deed does not warrant one of the gallantry medals. Around 1942, the commendations were extended to servicemen for gallantry where the deed did not warrant a gallantry medal. Publications of the persons name in the London Gazette and later the Canadian Gazette is needed to make a commendation official. Usually, only the names of the people are listed in the Gazette's but in the 1960s the Canada Gazette also had citations for the awards.

Description:

A plastic badge was issued to denote a civil commendation. The badge was gold with red, an eliptical wreath surmounted by a crown, with a sword running up the middle. In the centre in three lines are the words: FOR / BRAVE / CONDUCT. The badge is 40 mm high and 22 mm wide and was worn on a coat lapel.

The badge was changed to a silver oak leaf to allow servicemen to wear it on the appropriate ribbon or medal. The current medals have a brooch fitting to allow wearing on the coat lapel as well as on a ribbon or medal.

Issued:

KING's Commendations: 28

QUEEN's Commendations:

YEAR	RCAF	ARMY	RCN	CIVILIANS	YEAR	RCAF	ARMY	RCN	CIVILIANS
1952	4	1	1	0	1961	0	1	0	0
1953	1	1	1	0	1962	0	1	0	0
1954	3	4	0	0	1963	0	2	0	0
1955	1	1	2	0	1964	0	1	0	0
1956	3	2	1*	0	1965	0	2	3	2
1957	1	1	0	0	1966	1	8	3	6
1958	0	1	0	4	1967	3	1	2	0
1959	6	1	0	6	1968	1	1	4	6
1960	0	1	0	0	Total	25	31	16	24

Note: Replaced by the Canadian Bravery Decorations.

Examples:

Canada Gazette 28 October, 1967, Page 2677: The Minister of National Defence has announced that HER MAJESTY THE QUEEN has been graciously pleased to approve the following award: Queen's Commendation for Brave Conduct: SB 42458 Corporal HAROLD WILSON HUTCHINSON, C.D., The Fort Garry Horse: On June 28, 1967, Corporal Hutchinson was the non-commissioned officer in charge of the priming bay on the Grenade Range, at Sarcee Barracks, Calgary, Alberta. Whilst a soldier under his supervision was inserting a fuse in the grenade, the fuse commenced to burn. With complete disregard for his own personal safety, Corporal Hutchinson grasped the grenade from the soldier's hand and threw it out of the priming bay, thereby saving two soldiers from possible severe injury or death.

THE KING'S/QUEEN'S COMMENDATION FOR VALUABLE SERVICE IN THE AIR

Terms:
This award originated in 1942 to recognize meritorious civilian or service personnel in the air or to recognize gallantry not reaching the standard required for the Air Force Cross or the Air Force Medal.

Description:
Servicemen wear the Mentioned-in-Despatches emblem on the appropriate ribbon or if no medal is worn, on the jacket where ribbons are worn. Civilians wear a small eliptical (30mm high by 16mm wide) silver badge that has the words: FOR VALUABLE / SERVICE in two lines at the top.

Issued:
World War II to the RCAF; 297
Queen's Commendations to the RCAF: 1952 - 7 for Korea; 1953 - 6 for Korea plus 1; 1954 - 1; 1960 - 1; 1967 - 1:
Queen's Commendations to the RCN: 1953 - 1.

Examples:
Canada Gazette, 28 November 1953, Page 3545: The QUEEN has been graciously pleased to approve the following award: Queen's Commendation for Valuable Service in the Air: Lieutenant (P) Allan John Woods, 0-79575, RCN.

Canada Gazette, 16 September, 1967, page 2355: The Minister of National Defence has announced that HER MAJESTY THE QUEEN has been graciously pleased to approve the following awards:

Queen's Commendation for Brave Conduct — 54003 Flying Officer Robert John Veitch SIMPSON, Royal Canadian Air Force;

Queen's Commendation for Valuable Services in the Air — 82040 Flying Officer Joseph Thomas Serge Lorrain GAGNON, Royal Canadian Air Force;

While flying a United Nations Caribou aircraft on a flight from El Arish to Gaza on 17 May, 1967, Flying Officers Simpson and Gagnon were the pilot and co-pilot respectively. After entering the Gaza Strip they were harassed on three occasions by two Israeli fighter aircraft who, coming dangerously close, attempted to make the United Nations aircraft follow them into Israeli held territory. On one occasion several warning shots were fired. This harassment did not deter these officers who remained calm and determined, displaying sound judgement and professionalism, placing the safety of the aircraft and passengers foremost at all times. Although still followed by the two fighter aircraft, the United Nations aircraft was able to make a safe landing at the Gaza airstrip.

OBVERSES

The OBVERSE of a Medal is the side of the piece which generally carries the bust of the Sovereign or in the case of recent Canadian medals, a maple leaf. It is the side of the medal that when worn, is seen by others.

Since most of the medals described in this book are King George V, King George VI or Elizabeth II medals, this section will describe medals with these sovereigns' obverses.

GEORGE V

1911-1930:GEORGIVS V BRITT:OMN:REX ET IMP:

During this period, there was only one inscription around the edge and the following bust types with the medals using the type after. All are uncrowned in this era.

a) Field Marshall's Uniform:
   DCM, MM, MSM, Colonial Permanent Forces LS & GC, Colonial Auxiliary Forces LS & GC.
b) Admiral's Uniform:
   RCN LS & GC. (CGM & DSM if awarded would be this style)
c) Coinage Head:
   AFM, DFM, Edward Medal, King's Police Medal, ISM, RVM, British War Medal, Merchantile Marine War Medal.

1930-1937: GEORGIVS · V · D · G · BRITT · OMN REX · ET · INDIAE · IMP ·

This legend was introduced in 1930 with INDIAE replacing IND and D.G. added. All the medals issued in this era were crowned robed busts as per the photo of the King's Police and Fire Service Medal. Since there were no wars in this period, the only war medals (DCM, MM etc.) that would be awarded to Canadians would be replacement medals.

a) Crowned Robed Bust:
   MSM, King's Police and Fire Service Medal, RCMP LS Medal, Army LS & GC, Canadian Efficiency Medal. ISM.
b) Uncrowned Coinage:
   The RCN LS & GC medal of this era was the only one with the coinage head and had the legend of the 1911-1930 period.

These medals were issued during the brief reign of Edward VIII.

GEORGE VI

1937-1949: GEORGIVS VI D:G:BR:OMN:REX ET INDIAE IMP:

a) the following medals had this legend with a crowned head of George VI:
   DCM, CGM, GM, DSM, MM, ISM, King's Police & Fire Medal, Canada Medal, 39-45 War Medal, Army LS & GC Medal, Efficiency Medal.

GEORGIVS VI D:G:BR:OMN:REX F:D:IND:IMP.

b) The following medals had the uncrowned coinage head of George VI with the above legend; DFM, AFM, RVM, Polar Medal, Defence Medal, MSM, RCN LS & GC, RCAF LS & GC, Air Efficiency, RCNR LS & GC, RCNVR LS & GC, RCMP LS.

1949-1952: GEORGIVS VI DEI GRA:BRITT:OMN:REX FID:DEF:

a) India gained its independence and thus INDIAE & IND were dropped from the legend.

The following medals had the crowned head of George VI and were awarded during the early part of the Korean conflict:
DCM, DSM, GM, MM, ISM, King's Police & Fire Medal, Army LS,& GC, Efficiency Medal.

GEORGIVIS VI D:G:BRITT:OMN:REX FID:DEF:

b) The following medals had the uncrowned coinage head of George VI:
AFM, MSM, RVM, RCN LS & GC, RCAF LS & GC,RCNVR LS & GC, CD.

GEORGIVS VI DEI GRATIA REX

c) The RCMP LS Medal of this era had this shortened legend.

ELIZABETH II

1952-1953: ELIZABETH II D.G.:BR:OMN:REGINA F:D:

a) The following medals had the crowned, diademed bust:
DCM, GM, DSM, MM.

ELIZABETH II DEI GRA:BRITT:OMN:REGINA F:D:

b) The following medals had the uncrowned coinage head:
MSM,RVM, Polar Medal (to Taylor and Butson), RCN LS & GC, RCAF LS & GC.

1952-Present: ELIZABETH II DEI GRATIA REGINA · CANADA ·

a) The only two medals with this uncrowned coinage head legend are:
Canadian Korea Medal, Canadian Forces Decoration.

ELIZABETH II DEI GRATIA REGINA

b) The only medal with this uncrowned coinage head legend is:
RCMP Long Service Medal

c) The only medal with this crowned, diademed bust legend is:
Efficiency Medal

d) The only medal with this crowned, robed bust legend is:
Army Long Service Medal

1953-present:
The Queen's titles were altered on 28 May 1953 and the following legends began appearing on medals sometime in 1954.

ELIZABETH II DEI GRATIA REGINA F.D.

a) The following Medals with this crowned, diademed bust legend are:
George Medal, Queen's Medal for Champion Shot of the Army and for the RCAF. (note: British DCM's CGMs, DSMs, MMs, are now of this type but none of these has been awarded to a Canadian since the Korean War).

ELIZABETH II · DEI · GRATIA · REGINA · F:D: ·

b) The medals with this uncrowned coinage head legend are:
MSM, RCN LS & GC, RCAF LS & GC.

ELIZABETH II DEI GRATIA REGINA FID:DEF:

c) The only medal with this uncrowned, coinage head is: AFM

ELIZABETH II DEI GRATIA REGINA FID · DEF ·

d) The only medal with this crowned, diademed bust legend is:
Efficiency Medal.

CANADIAN MILITARY HONOUR POLICY — 1980

PURPOSE:

To define national policy governing decorations and medals for members of the Canadian Forces.

DEFINITIONS:

Honours means Orders, Decorations or Medals emanating from the Queen through the Governor General.

Order means a society of honour established to recognize outstanding achievement or service.

Decoration means an honour bestowed to recognize: Bravery in military operations against an armed enemy; or bravery in situations not involving military operations against an armed enemy; or outstanding achievement in a particular activity.

Medal means an honour bestowed to recognize: war service in a theatre of active operations; or service under exceptional circumstances not in a theatre of active operations; or commemoration of a special occasion or anniversary at the national level; or long service and good conduct.

Minister means the Minister of National Defence.

CATEGORIES OF HONOURS WHICH MAY BE CONSIDERED

The Government recognizes that Canadian honours should fall into the categories listed below, and if the circumstances are deemed appropriate, will consider proposals from the Minister regarding institution of individual honours within these categories.

ORDER

Merit: For outstanding achievement or service.

Bravery: a) in active combat in the face of an armed enemy. For bravery above and beyond the call of duty in military operations against an armed enemy.

b) not in the face of an armed enemy. For bravery involving risk of life or limb in situations not involving military operations against an armed enemy.

Outstanding Professional Achievement: For demonstrating exceptional professional skill in a specific activity.

MEDALS

War Service: For military service in a clearly defined locality for a specific duration to recognize service in a theatre of active operations.

General Service: For military service in a clearly defined locality for a specified duration to recognize service under exceptional circumstances not necessarily in a theatre of active operations.

Commemmorative: For participation in a special occasion or anniversary at the national level.

Long Service and Good Conduct: For completion of a prescribed period of service under terms of efficiency and conduct.

GUIDELINES FOR INSTITUTING HONOURS

Proposals for instituting honours must satisfy the demands of the following factors:

Respect: Fundamental to the concept of honours is that they carry prestige. Their raison d'etre is to recognize an accomplishment commanding the respect of members of the military, the general public and the person honoured.

Equitability: Non-recognition of this factor could produce the negative effect of dissatisfaction rather than improve morale. If an honour is bestowed for duty under certain circumstances, similar kinds of duty and circumstances should also be rewarded.

Credibility: This factor is related to respect. To be credible, an honour must represent a worthy endeavour. It must not represent routine duty.

PROCEDURES FOR INSTITUTING HONOURS

Any proposal to institute an honour shall be submitted to the Government Committee on Honours Policy which will make recommendations to the Minister. On advice from the committee, the Minister may submit a memorandum to Cabinet requesting the Prime Minister to petition the Queen for approval to make an appropriate Order in Council.

SEQUENCE FOR WEARING CANADIAN ORDERS, DECORATIONS AND MEDALS
(1972 Guide)

This sequence is for those awarded medals after 1 June 1972. Those awards received before 1 June 1972 have a different sequence with the Victoria Cross taking precedence. Thus Dr. Richard Buston wears his George Cross before his Officer of the Order of Military Merit and Roy Flake, DSO, DFC, SC wears his Star of Courage after his DFC. There are unlikely to be many more of these anomalies and thus the current sequence will be that normally used. The Chancellory is reviewing this listing and could alter some anomalies such as an Officer of the Order of Canada taking precedence over a Commander of the Order of Military Merit and the Medal of Bravery taking precedence over Members of the Orders of Canada and Military Merit (normally a medal does not take precedence over an order). The Royal Victorian Order must also be reviewed and likely in the revised list, Commanders of this Order will come after the Order of Canada with other grades being appropriately positioned. The Order of Merit may also come after the Order of Canada as it is the Sovereigns personal gift as opposed to being a foreign (British) award. I have guessed at where the Meritorious Service Cross fits in this sequence and it too will have to be positioned better in a revision to this list.

Cross of Valour	Star of Courage
Companion of the Order of Canada	Officer of the Order of Military Merit
Officer of the Order of Canada	Medal of Bravery
Commander of the Order of Military Merit	Member of the Order of Canada
	Member of the Order of Military Merit

Meritorious Service Cross
Victoria Cross
George Cross
Order of Merit
Order of the Companions of Honour
Companion of the Order of the Bath
Companion of the Order of St. Michael
and St.George
Commander of the Royal Victorian
Order
Commander of the Order of the British
Empire
Distinguished Service Order
Lieutenant of the Royal Victorian
Order
Officer of the Order of the British
Empire
Imperial Service Order
Member of the Royal Victorian Order
Member of the Order of the British
Empire
Member of the Royal Red Cross
Distiguished Service Cross
Military Cross
Distinguished Flying Cross
Air Force Cross
Associate of the Royal Red Cross
Order of St. John (All Grades)
Distinguished Conduct Medal
Conspicuous Gallantry Medal
George Medal
Distinguished Service Medal
Military Medal
Distinguished Flying Medal
Air Force Medal
British Empire Medal

War Medals (as per sequence in book)
Canadian Korean War Medal
Special Services Medal
United Nations Medals (as per
sequence in book)
ICSC Medal
ICCS Medal
Polar Medal
Royal Victorian Medal

Commemorative Medals (as per book
except)
Elizabeth II Coronation Medal
Centennial Medal
Elizabeth II Silver Jubilee Medal
Canadian Medal for Long Service and
Good Conduct
Naval Long Service and Good Conduct
Medal
Air Force Long Service and Good
Conduct Medal
Royal Canadian Mounted Police Long
Service Medal
Police Exemplary Service Medal
Corrections Exemplary Service Medal
(Firefighters Exemplary Service Medal)
(Coast Guard Exemplary Service
Medal)
Volunteer Officer's Decoration
Volunteer Long Service Medal
Colonial Auxiliary Forces Officer's
Decoration
Colonial Auxiliary Forces Long
Service Medal
Efficiency Decoration
Efficiency Medal
Naval Volunteer Reserve Decoration
Naval Volunteer Reserve LS & GC
Medal
Air Efficiency Award

Queen's Medal for Champion Shots

Canadian Forces Decoration

Service Medal of the Order of St. John

Orders, Decorations & Medals of other
Commonwealth Members

Foreign Awards — Orders,
Decorations and Medals each in the
order awarded.

Royal Humane Society (worn on the
right breast)
Royal Canadian Humane Society
Life Saving Medal of the Order of St.
John

MEDAL PRICES

As noted in the introduction on page 1, medal prices vary considerably depending on several factors. In establishing a price, these factors must be taken into consideration:

1. **The condition of a medal** — the general terms used are: Mint; EF (Extremely Fine); VF (Very Fine); F (Fine); Worn or poor. In general, be careful in buying medals that are not EF or VF.

2. **Naming** — if to a Canadian, the rank (officers usually more costly than to a man), the unit and number to that unit if the medal can be verified. Medals named for persons of importance, or for a particular battle of which medals are few in number, will be accordingly higher in price.

3. **Bars or clasps** increase the value.

The prices indicated here are for EF, single medals, with a column for Canadian medals and a column for their British equivalent. The Canadian 1939-45 War Medal is made of silver and therefore is more valuable than the cupro-nickel British equivalent. A Military Medal (M.M.) to a Canadian is considered more valuable than a British M.M. because fewer were awarded. Where it is unlikely a medal will be available for sale, the number is put in brackets.

There are many copies on the market and some of these are of very high quality. Where I know of the existence of copies, I have marked the British price with an asterisk (*). There are also many unnamed specimens that are not copies but because they are unnamed cost considerably less than named medals — these have been included in the price lists. I have included a column which indicates if the medals were originally issued unnamed, named or are numbered. The letters are used as follows:
U - Unnamed; N - Named; # - Numbered.

No.	MEDAL		Level/King	Canadian	British	Miniature
1.	Order of Canada	#	Companion	6,200.00	—	40.00
		#	Officer	2,750.00	—	40.00
		#	Member	1,500.00	—	35.00
2.	Order of Military Merit	#	Commander	5,000.00	—	35.00
		#	Officer	3,500.00	—	35.00
		#	Member	1,800.00	—	35.00
3.	Cross of Valour	#		(14)	—	35.00
4.	Star of Courage	N		4,000.00	—	30.00
5.	Medal of Bravery	N		2,500.00	*	25.00
6.	Medal of Courage	#		(0)	—	—
7.	Medal of Service	#		4,000.00	—	—
8.	Canada Medal			(0)	—	—
9.	Order of Merit	#		(3)	10,000.00	?
10.	Order of Companions of Honour	#		(7)	4,000.00	?
11.	Order of the Bath	U	Companion	‡1,500.00 +	400.00	35.00
12.	Order of St. Michael and St. George	U	Companion	‡1,500.00 +	375.00	35.00
13.	Royal Victorian Order	#	Commander	1,000.00 +	275.00	35.00
		#	Member	800.00 +	200.00	30.00
	Royal Victorian Medal	U	Edward VII	‡350.00 +	145.00	20.00
		U	George V	‡250.00 +	120.00	20.00
		U	George VI	‡350.00 +	150.00	25.00

‡must be verified & attributed through other named medals in a group.

No.	MEDAL		Level/King	Canadian	British	Miniature
14.	Royal Victorian Chain	U	—	(2)	—	—
15.	Imperial Service Order	U	George V	‡250.00 +	125.00	30.00
16.	Imperial Service Medal	N	George V	75.00	25.00	15.00
		N	George VI	60.00	25.00	15.00
		N	E II R	60.00	25.00	15.00
17.	Order of the British Empire	U	Commander (1)	‡350.00 +	200.00	20.00
		U	Commander (2)	‡350.00 +	200.00	20.00
		U	Officer (1)	‡150.00 +	75.00	15.00
		U	Officer (2)	‡150.00 +	75.00	15.00
		U	Member (1)	‡100.00 +	70.00	15.00
		U	Member (2)	‡100.00 +	70.00	15.00
18.	Order of St. John	U	Knight (set)	200.00	200.00	15.00
		U	Commander	125.00	125.00	15.00
		U	Officer	100.00	100.00	15.00
		U	Serving Brother	75.00	75.00	15.00
19.	Victoria Cross	N		25,000.00 +	15,000.00*	20.00
20.	George Cross	N		30,000.00 +	5,000.00*	20.00
21.	Distinguished Service Order	U	George V	‡750.00	325.00	30.00
22.	Royal Red Cross	U	George V	‡500.00	175.00	25.00
		U	George VI	‡600.00	175.00	25.00
		U	E II RR	(1)	175.00	25.00
	Associate Royal Red Cross	U	George V	‡300.00	90.00	20.00
		U	George VI	‡400.00	170.00	20.00
		U	E II R	(1)	125.00	20.00
23.	Distinguished Service Cross	U	George V	‡1000.00	350.00*	20.00
		U	George VI	‡1,800.00 +	500.00*	20.00
24.	Military Cross	U	George V	‡400.00	200.00*	20.00
		U	George VI	‡800.00	325.00	20.00
25.	Distinguished Flying Cross	U	George VI	‡600.00	400.00*	25.00
26.	Air Force Cross	U	George VI	‡900.00	500.00*	25.00
27.	George Medal	N	George VI	2,200.00	600.00	20.00
		N	Elizabeth II	3,500.00	800.00	20.00
28.	Distinguished Conduct Medal	N	George V	450.00 +	175.00	15.00
		N	George VI	2,500.00 +	500.00	15.00
	Unnamed Specimen	U	George VI	150.00	—	15.00
29.	Distinguished Service Medal	N	George V	1000.00	525.00	15.00
		N	George VI	1000.00	400.00	15.00
30.	Military Medal	N	George V	175.00	100.00	15.00
		N	George VI	800.00	400.00	15.00
	Unnamed Specimen	U	George VI	150.00	—	15.00
31.	Distinguished Flying Medal	N	George VI	1,600.00	500.00*	15.00
32.	Air Force Medal	N	George VI	4,500.00	700.00*	15.00
33.	Conspicuous Gallantry Medal	N	George VI	7,500.00	4,500.00	15.00
34.	British Empire Medal	U	George VI	‡275.00	100.00*	15.00
35.	Empire Gallantry Medal	U	George VI	—	—	15.00
36.	Albert Medal	N		5,000.00	900.00	50.00
37.	Edward Medal	N	George V	—	900.00	20.00
38.	Military General Service Medal	N	Chateauguay	2,200.00	—	125.00
			Chrystler	2,500.00	—	125.00
			Fort Detroit	2,200.00	—	125.00
39.	Canadian General Service Medal	N	F.R. 1866	165.00	—	50.00
		N	F.R. 1870	220.00	—	50.00

No.	MEDAL	Level/King	Canadian	British	Miniature
		N	R.R. 1870	1,100.00	—	50.00
	Unnamed Specimens	U	1 bar/2 bars	125.00	—	50.00
40.	Egypt Medal 1884 - 1885	N	Nile 1884-85	2,000.00	135.00	30.00
		N	Nile and Kirbekan	2,200.00	—	30.00
		N	No Bar	1,700.00	75.00	30.00
41.	Khedive's Bronze Star	U		‡45.00	35.00	—
42.	Pontifical Zouaves Volunteer	U		200.00	—	—
43.	North West Canada	N	No Bar	350.00	—	50.00
		N	Saskatchewan	700.00	—	85.00
		U	unnamed	200.00	—	50.00
44.	Queen's South Africa Medal	N		450.00	60.00	22.00
	Awards to Lord Strathcona					
	Horse with Bars (raised dates)	N		4,500.00	—	15.00
45.	King's South Africa Medal	N	2 bars	3,500.00	35.00	15.00
46.	1914 Star	N		750.00	30.00	8.00
	with bar			1,000.00	40.00	—
47.	1914 - 1915 Star	N		12.00	8.00	5.00
48.	British War Medal	N		15.00	12.00	5.00
49.	Victory Medal	N		8.00	3.00	5.00
50.	Mercantile Marine War Medal	N		‡50.00	20.00	5.00
51.	1939 - 1945 Star	U	no bar	5.00	5.00	5.00
52.	Atlantic Star	U	no bar	18.00	18.00*	5.00
53.	Air Crew Europe Star	U	no bar	100.00	100.00*	5.00
54.	Africa Star	U	no bar	8.00	8.00	5.00
55.	Pacific Star	U	no bar	15.00	15.00	5.00
56.	Burma Star	U	no bar	12.00	12.00	5.00
57.	Italy Star	U		7.00	7.00	5.00
58.	France and Germany Star	U	no bar	9.00	9.00	5.00
	Bars to above stars	U	Original/Copy	3.00	3.00*	3.00
59.	Defence Medal	U		16.00	5.00	7.00
60.	Cdn. Volunteer Service Medal	U	no bar	20.00	—	7.00
		U	with bar	25.00	— *	7.00
61.	1939 - 1945 War Medal	U		15.00	5.00	7.00
62.	Canadian Korean War Medal	N		90.00	50.00*	7.00
63.	U.N. Service Medal - Korea	N		25.00	15.00*	7.00
64.	U.N. Emergency Force (UNEF)	U		50.00	30.00*	7.00
65. to 75.	United Nations Medals *Same Medal for all with different ribbons*	U		45.00 +	30.00*	7.00
76.	I.C.S.C. Indo China 1967	U		175.00	100.00*	15.00
77.	I.C.C.S. Viet Nam 1973	U		250.00	150.00*	15.00
78.	Champion Shot of Canadian Army	N		450.00	150.00	15.00
79.	Champion Shot of the R.C.A.F.	N		(12)	350.00	15.00
80.	Queen Victoria Diamond Jubilee	U		‡300.00 +	110.00	20.00
81.	King Edward VII Coronation	U		‡250.00 +	75.00	20.00
82.	King George V Coronation	U		‡50.00 +	25.00	15.00
83.	King George V Jubilee	U		30.00	25.00	15.00
84.	King George VI Coronation	U		30.00	25.00	15.00
85.	Queen Elizabeth Coronation	U		45.00	25.00*	15.00
86.	Queen Elizabeth Jubilee	U		85.00	— *	15.00

No.	MEDAL	Level/King		Canadian	British	Miniature
87.	Canadian Centennial Medal	U		85.00	— *	12.00
88.	Polar Medals	N		(17)	—	20.00
89.	Canadian Forces Decoration	N	George VI	75.00	— *	8.00
		N	E II R	40.00	— *	5.00
90.	Canadian Medal LS & GC	N	George V	175.00	—	15.00
		N	George VI	175.00	—	15.00
		N	E II R	200.00	—	16.00
91.	Colonial Perm. Forces LS & GC	N	George V	375.00	—	15.00
92.	Long Service & Good Conduct 1901	N	Edward VII	400.00	35.00	15.00
93.	R.C.N. L.S. & G.C.	N	George V	400.00	40.00	15.00
		N	George VI	400.00	35.00	15.00
		N	E II R	500.00	35.00	15.00
94.	R.C.A.F. L.S. & G.C.	N	George VI	400.00	75.00	15.00
95.	Air Efficiency Award	N	George VI	300.00	135.00	15.00
96.	Canadian Efficiency Decoration	N	George VI	175.00	—	15.00
97.	Canadian Efficiency Medal	N	George V	165.00	—	15.00
		N	George VI	110.00	—	15.00
		N	E II R	190.00	—	15.00
98.	Col. Auxiliary Officers Dec.	N	Victoria	300.00	—	25.00
		N	Edward	400.00	—	25.00
		N	George V	225.00	—	25.00
99.	Col. Auxiliary Forces LS & GC	N	George V	150.00	—	18.00
100.	Meritorious Service Medal	N	George V	200.00	65.00	15.00
		N	George VI	275.00	75.00	15.00
101.	R.C.N.V.R. Officer's Decor.	U	George VI	‡400.00	175.00	15.00
102.	R.C.N.V.R. L.S. & G.C.	N	George VI	500.00	40.00	15.00
	Unnamed Specimen	U	George VI	55.00	55.00	15.00
103.	R.C.N. (R) Officer's Decor.	U	George VI	‡300.00	150.00	15.00
104.	R.C.N. (R) L.S. & G.C.	N	George VI	700.00	40.00	15.00
105.	Service Medal, Order of St. John	N	Victoria	30.00	25.00	15.00
106.	RCMP Long Service Medal	N	E II R	400.00	—	12.00
107.	King's Police Service Medal	N	George VI	1,500.00	450.00	15.00
108.	Police Exemplary Service Medal			**	—	—
109.	Corrections Exemplary Service Medal			**	—	—
110.	Meritorious Service Cross			**	—	—
111.	Special Service Medal			**	—	—
112.	Memorial Cross		GV	30.00	—	—
	Memorial Cross		GVI	65.00 +	—	—
113.	Firefighter Exemplary Service Medal			**	—	—
114.	Coast Guard Exemplary Service Medal			**	—	—

**The new Canadian medals have not been available long enough to establish a price.

OTHER MILITARY TITLES AVAILABLE
FROM THE UNITRADE PRESS
Canadian Reference Books and Catalogues

Canada's Army in World War II — The Badges & Histories of the Corps and Regiments, 3rd Edition by F.R. Tripp. This book catalogues and illustrates the badges of the Canadian Army as it existed during the years of the second world war. It provides a concise history of service records of the corps and regiments as well as their major battle honours. The 3rd edition has added the divisions that didn't see service overseas and the badges of the Canadian Officer Training Corps. The 3rd edition also includes up-to-date prices for all badges listed! 120 pp, over 200 illus, PB. $8.95*

Canadian Expeditionary Force Military Cap Badges of World War I, A. Rosen & P. Martin. 1985 edition includes both the Expeditionary and Battalion Badges. Over 330 badges are described, illustrated and valued, with over 700 badge types described and valued. 125 pp, over 500 illus, PB. 7.50*

Cap Badges of the Canadian Expeditionary Force 1914-1919, Babin. For over 25 years this has been the standard reference work. 42 pp, illus, CC. 4.95*

Canadian Cap Badges of World War I, Chris Brooker. A price guide companion to Babins "Cap Badges of the Cdn Expeditionary Force". 21 pp, CC. 4.95*

Canadian Cap Badges of World War II, Chris Brooker. A price guide companion to all badges listed in "Canada's Army in World War II". 2nd edition, 29 pp, illus, CC. 4.95*

The Concise Lineages of the Canadian Army, 1855 to date, C. Stewart. Completely revised. Includes dates of organization, designations, amalgamations, dates of disbandment, battle honours, uniform details and much more. 193 pp, illus, PB, Large Format. . . . . 19.95†

The Canadian Medal Rolls - The Distinguished Flying Medal (1939-1945), M. Ashton. 102 pp, illus, PB. 14.95*

The Canadian Medal Rolls - Distinguished Conduct and Military Medal (1939-45 & 1950-53), M. Ashton. 129 pp, illus, PB. 14.95*

The Medal Roll of the Red River Campaign of 1870 in Canada, G. Neale. 70 pp, illus, HB. 19.95*

Orders, Decorations and Medals

The Medals Yearbook, 6th Edition, D. Collins & N. Nix. Price guide with very accurate market prices. Covers gallantry awards, campaign, long-service, etc. Includes 15 new medal write-ups and "Order of Precedence". 140 pp, illus, HB. . . . . 19.95†

Spink's Catalogue of British and Associated Orders, Decorations and Medals with Valuations, E.C. Joslin. The authoritative guide. Includes a brief history of each, illustration, and valuations. Latest (1983) edition. 192 pp, illus (incl. 70 colour), HB. . . . 39.95†

Ribbons and Medals, Taprell Dorling. New edition. Completely revised. First published in 1916, this has become the benchmark on the subject. This edition has been masterfully revised and edited by Alec Purves. Over 550 life-size photos with 24 colour pages for ribbons. 334 pp, illus, HB. . 39.95*

Orders, Medals and Decorations of Britain and Europe, P. Hieronymussen. A comprehensive survey of civilian and military decorations from 29 European countries. 450 examples are illustrated in 80 pages of photos printed in superb 7-colour lithography. Military decorations include examples of those worn in World War II. 256 pp, illus, HB. 14.95*

The Queen's South Africa Medal to the Royal Navy and the Royal Marines, W.H. Fevyer & J.W. Wilson. Complete listing includes all bar combinations, returned medals, casualties, killed, POW's, a numerical breakdown and analysis by ships, bars and bars per medal. 148 pp, illus, HB. 48.95†

The Medals, Decorations & Orders of the Great War 1914-1918, Alec Purves. This book covers all the orders, decorations and medals instituted by the Allies, the Central Powers, neutral countries and the emergent nations, during or in connection with the war. Over 150 ribbons in full colour, 95 photos and several line drawings. 199 pp, HB. . . . . 18.50†

The Observer's Book of British Awards and Medals, E.C. Joslin. 192 pp, illus incl. 8 colour plates and ribbon charts, HB. . . . 7.95*

The George Medal (1940-1945), W.H. Fevyer. 114 pp, illus, PB. . . . . 24.95†

The History of the Order of the Bath and its Insignia, J.C. Risk. 150 pp, 25 b/w plates & 3 colour plates, HB. . . . . 21.95†

The Distinguished Service Medal 1914-1920, W.H. Fevyer. A complete record of all DSM's awarded for the first World War Period. 121 pp, illus, HB. . . . . . . 49.95†

Medal Rolls: 23rd Foot - Royal Welch Fusiliers, Napoleonic Period, N. Holme & E.L.Kirby. 206 pp, 5 b/w plates, HB. . 33.95†

Dragon's Can Be Defeated, D.V. Henderson. A complete record of the George Medal's progress from 1940 to 1983. 120 pp, illus, HB. Large Format. . . . . 32.50†

Spink Medal Booklets, J.M.A. Tamplin. This series documents the recipients, giving name, rank, serial number, regiment and the date of the award. Illustrates the medal it describes. Excellent

No. 1 - **The Imperial Yeomanry Long Service and Good Conduct Medal.** 1978, 52 pp, CC. . . . . 7.95†

No. 2 - **The Militia Long Service and Good Conduct Medal.** 52 pp, CC. . 10.95†

No. 3 - **The Special Reserve Long Service and Good Conduct Medal,** 40 pp, CC. 11.95†

No. 4 - **The Volunteer Officer's Decoration.** 1980, 48 pp, 16 illus, CC. . . . . 11.95†

No. 5 - **Volunteer Long Service Medals.** 1981, 48 pp, 10 illus, CC. . . 14.95†

No. 6 - **The Colonial Auxiliary Forces Officers Decoration: Indian Volunteer Forces Decoration,** 1981, 88 pp, 9 illus, CC. . . 19.95†

No. 7 - **The Territorial Decoration 1908-1930.** 1983, 68 pp, 8 plates, CC. . . . . 19.95†

No. 8 - **Colonial Auxiliary Forces Long Service Medal.** 1984, 88 pp, 10 illus, CC. . . . . 19.95†

The Army of India Medal Roll 1799-1826, Hayward. 123 pp, HB. . . . . 22.50†

The Meritorious Service Medal to Naval Forces, Ian McInnes. The medal rolls. 63 pp, illus, CC. . . . . 14.95†

Recipients fo the Distinguished Conduct Medal 1855-1909, P.E. Abbott. The definitive work in this field, lists all DCMs awarded, campaign by campaign, together with relevant information. 112 pp, 5 illus, HB. Large Format. . . . . 21.95†

The Distinguished Service Order 1886-1923, Sir O. Creagh & E.M. Humphris. Contains citations and biographical notes on all recipients of the DSO from 1886-1923. 815 pp, 1049 illus HB. Large Format. . 74.95†

British Campaign Medals: Waterloo to the Falklands, R.W. Gould. This ideal introduction and reference guide contains over 100 life-sized illustrations. Each medal and ribbon is realistically priced. 80 pp, illus, HB. 14.95*

Collecting Medals and Decorations, A.A. Purves. Provides notes on naming - genuine and false, unofficial bars, copies, etc. Includes info on housing the collection, buying and selling, building a reference library and identifying abbreviations of rank and unit. Excellent. 237 pp, illus, HB. . . . 24.95†

British Gallantry Awards, P.E. Abbott & J.M.A. Tamplin. 2nd edition. Each medal is described in detail including the variations, the Warrants, numbers awarded and examples of specific citations. 359 pp, illus, HB. . . . . 47.95†

The Iron Cross: A History 1813-1957, G. Williamson. Traces the history and design of the Iron Cross from its first award in 1813. Includes notes on the principal recipients, info on grades, award documents, restoring, fakes, etc. Listing of current values. 175 pp, 184 illus, HB. 16.95*

Insignia & Badges

Formation Badges of World War II: Britain, Commonwealth and Empire, H. Cole. The standard reference work on the subject, out of print for over 10 years. It records, describes and illustrates every formation badge and sign involved in W.W. II (over 500). It includes details of the different campaigns and garrisons in which the formations served; a guide to distinguishing letters; indexes of formations. 192 pp, 500 illus (4 pages colour), HB. Large Format. . . 20.95*

British Army Cloth Insignia 1940 to the Present, B.L. Davis. Lavishly illustrated. Describes, illustrates and values over 600 badges. Includes: formation badges; shoulder-strap titles; regimental and corps designations, flashes and airborne insignia; rank and insignia, and much more! 68 pp, over 600 illus, HB. 13.95*

Glengarry Badges of the British Line Regiments to 1881, W. Y. Carman. With over 150 illustrations, this is the definitive collectors guide to pre-territorial badges. 64 pp, illus, HB. 13.95*

Badges of the British Army 1820-1960, F. Wilkinson. The most popular guide to badge collecting, now with a 1984/85 price guide. 76 pp, illus, HB. 13.95*

Scottish Regimental Badges 1793-1971, including Commonwealth Forces, W.H. & K.D. Bloomer. A revised edition of this illustrated reference guide, complete with 1982/83 price guide.
88 pp, over 500 illus, HB. 13.95*

Buttons of the British Army 1855-1970, H. Ripley. Illustrated guide with price guide.
72 pp, 670 illus, HB. 13.95*

Naval and Marine Badges and Insignia of World War II, G. Rosignoli. Illustrates in full colour 1360 badges and insignia. Includes Britain, USSR, Denmark, Germany, France, Italy, USA, Japan, Poland, Netherlands and Finland. 167 pp, 64 pages colour & 6 b/w, HB. 17.50*

Army Badges and Insignia of World War II, G. Rosignoli. Illustrates over 2000 badges and insignia of the principal armed forces of WW II. 228 pp, 80 pages colour, HB. . 14.95*

Army Badges and Insignia Since 1945, G. Rosignoli. Nearly 2000 badges and insignia are depicted in full colour, representing all the world's major fighting forces. 218 pp, 88 pages colour & 5 b/w, HB. 12.95*

Parachute Badges and Insignia of the World, B. Campbell & Reynolds. Includes histories of the units, descriptions of the uniforms and colour illustrations of over 2000 badges of the marines, commandos and naval infantrymen of the world. 160 pp, 49 colour plates, HB. 22.50*

Badges and Insignia of the Third Reich 1933-1945, B.L. Davis. Includes not only badges, but also emblems, shoulder straps and collar patches, cuff titles, arm bands, Chevrons and sleeve-rings, arm shields and much more! Covers the armed forces, political organizations, civilian groups, occupied countries, etc. 160 pp, full colour, HB. Large Format. 23.95*

World Army Badges and Insignia Since 1939, G. Rosignoli. Over 4000 badges and insignia in full colour! Text provides notes on how they were won.
448 pp, colour illus, HB. 22.50*

Uniforms

World Army Uniforms 1939 to the Present, Mollo, McGregor and Smith. Single volume combination of "Army Uniforms of World War II" and "Army Uniforms Since 1945". Covers the uniforms, weapons, and personal equipment of the 24 nations that took part in WW II. Full introduction and campaign details. 352 pp, 96 pages colour, PB. 17.50*

Army Uniforms of World War I, A. Mollo. The peace-time and field uniforms of all army and aviation services that fought in WWI. Includes badges, coats, foot and headgear and personal equipment along with indications of rank. 220 pp, colour illus, HB. 12.95*

Army Uniforms of World War II, A. Mollo & McGregor. 183 pp, colour illus, HB. 12.95*

Army Uniforms Since 1945, D. Smith. 176 pp, 48 pages colour, 27 b/w, PB. 8.95*

British Military Uniforms 1768-96, H. Strachan. 384 pp, illus, HB. 27.95*

British Army Uniforms & Insignia of World War Two, B.L. Davis. Description and illustrations of each item of wear for the Army 1935-1945. 276 pp, 850 b/w illus & 4 pages colour, HB. Large Format. 27.95*

Uniforms Illustrated, Arms and Armour Press.

No. 1 - US Special Forces of World War II, L. Thompson. 8.50*
No. 2 - The Modern British Soldier, S. Dunstan. 8.50*
No. 3 - US Special Forces 1945 to the Present, L. Thompson. 8.50*
No. 4 - The British Army in Northern Ireland, S. Dunstan. 8.50*
No. 5 - German Combat Uniforms of World War Two, B.L. Davis. 8.50*
No. 6 - Nato Uniforms Todays, D. Smith 8.50*
No. 7 - German Combat Uniforms of World War Two, Volume Two, B.L. Davis 8.50*
No. 8 - Soviet Army Uniforms Today, S. J. Zaloga. 8.50*
No. 9 - Soviet Army Uniforms of WWII, S.J. Zaloga. 8.50*
No. 10 - The Paras - The British Parachute Regiment, Shortt. 8.50*

*Note: this is a paperback series with each at least 64 pages and some colour & b/w photos.

Uniforms of the French Foreign Legion 1831-1981, Martin Windrow. 160 pp, 32 pages colour, HB. 27.95*

Uniforms of the French Revolutionary Wars 1789-1802. P.J. Haythornthwaithe. 160 pp, 64 pages colour, HB. 27.95*

Uniforms of Waterloo in Colour, P.J. Haythornthwaithe. 190 pp, 80 pages colour, HB. 12.95*

Uniforms of the Imperial Russian Army, B. Mollo. 160 pp, 64 pages colour, HB. 18.50*

British Cavalry Uniforms Since 1660, Barthorp. 24.95*

The Indian Army, B. Mollo. Traces history of the Indian Army, illustrating uniforms from early Sepoys through Guides and Gurkas. Status of Indian regiments, successor units, etc. 192 pp, colour & b/w photos, HB. Large Format. 33.50*

Weapons

Swords and Daggers, F. Wilkinson. Covers over 300 items that the collector is most likely to encounter, identified and priced. 80 pp, illus, HB. 14.95*

World Bayonets, 1800 to the Present, A. Carter. A reliable reference to the current values of the most frequently encountered bayonets. 72 pp, illus, HB. 14.95*

Revolvers, 1870-1940, I.V. Hogg. Offers a selection of guns that cover every type, class and range of revolver. Includes pricing. 72 pp, illus, HB. 14.95*

Sporting Guns, F. Wilkinson. Includes terms, features, accessories and collecting tips. 80 pp, illus, HB. 14.95*

The German Rifle, J. Walter. A comprehensive history of the standard boltaction designs 1871-1945. 160 pp, illus, HB. 17.95*

Weapons and Equipment of the Napoleonic Wars, P.J. Haythornwaithe. 190 pp, illus, HB. Large Format. 33.50*

Weapons and Equipment of the Victorian Soldier, D. Featherstone. 130 pp, illus, HB. Large Format. 25.95*

Weapons and Equipment of the Falklands Conflict, Perre H. 8.95*

Antique Firearms, F. Wilkinson. 276 pp, illus, HB. Large Format. 32.95*

The Official Price Guide to Pocket Knives, Pocket price guide. 276 pp, illus, PB. 5.50*

The Official Price Guide to Collector Guns, Domestic and Foreign handguns, rifles and shotguns. Pocket price guide. 267 pp, illus, PB. 6.95*

The Official Price Guide to Collector Handguns. Over 5500 market values for handguns of every type. Detailed listings including assembly diagrams for many models. 536 pp, illus, PB. 16.95*

The Official Price Guide to Collector Handguns. Over 5500 market values for handguns of every type. 536 pp, illus PB. 16.95*

The Official Price Guide to Collector Knives. Over 14,000 market values. Identification guide. 728 pp, illus, PB. ... 14.95*

The Official Price Guide to Antique and Modern Firearms. 32,000 market values. Covers handguns, rifles, shotguns, automatic weapons. 653 pp, illus, PB. 14.94*

Military History

Terriors in the Trenches, C. Messenger. The story of the Post Office Rifles at war 1914-1918. 170 pp, illus, HB. .... 26.95†

Warneford, V.C. - The First Naval Airman to be Awarded the V.C., M. Gibson. 128 pp, illus, HB. .... 17.95†

Operation SKUA, Major R.T. Partridge. Fascinating account of this battle. 159 pp, illus, HB. .... 16.50†

The Hawks: A Short History of the 14th/King's Hussars, B. Perrett. 151 pp, illus, HB. .... 29.95†

The Rifle Volunteers 1859-1908, R. Westlake. 173 pp, illus, HB. 21.50*

Gunfire in Barbary, R. Perkins & K.V. Douglas-Morris. The story of Admiral Lord Exmouth's battle with the Corsairs of Algiers in 1816. 200 pp, illus, HB. .. 29.95†

The Great Raids: Peenemunde, 17th August 1943, J. Searby. 84 pp, illus, PB. Large Format .... 12.95†

The Great Raids: Essen, March 1943-Battle of the Ruhr, J. Searby. 93 pp, illus, PB. Large Format. .... 12.95†

The Kashmir Gate, Lieutenant Duncan Home and the Delhi VCs, R. Perkins. 29.95*

General Militaria

The Official Price Guide to Military Collectibles. The largest comprehensive list of military objects available, 15th century to date. Over 12,000 prices, with advice on buying and selling. 565 pp, illus, PB. 14.95*

The Official Price Guide to Military Collectibles, Pocket Edition. Over 4000 current prices for a wide assortment of military objects, 19th century to World War II. 228 pp, illus, PB. 3.95*

The Official Price Guide to Collectibles of the Third Reiche. Over 4100 current prices for all types of 3rd Reiche items. 280 pp,illus, PB. 15.50*

Till The Boys Come Home, Tonie and Valmi Holt. The picture postcards of the First World War. Over 700 cards illustrated in b/w and colour. 192 pp, illus, HB. 24.95†

These titles can be ordered through your local dealer or bookstore or directly from The Unitrade Press. Orders to Unitrade should include $1.50 per order for postage and handling. **The Unitrade Press,** 127 Cartwright Avenue, Toronto, Ontario. M6A 1V4.

SEQUENCE FOR WEARING RIBBONS OF ORDERS, DECORATIONS AND MEDALS

VICTORIA CROSS / CROIX DE VICTORIA	**GEORGE CROSS** / CROIX DE GEORGE	**CROSS OF VALOUR** / CROIX DE LA VAILLANCE	**COMPANION OF THE ORDER OF CANADA** / COMPAGNON DE L'ORDRE DU CANADA	**OFFICER OF THE ORDER OF CANADA** / OFFICIER DE L'ORDRE DU CANADA	**ORDER OF MERIT** / ORDRE DU MÉRITE
DISTINGUISHED SERVICE ORDER / ORDRE DU SERVICE DISTINGUÉ	**ROYAL VICTORIAN ORDER MEMBER OF THE FOURTH CLASS** / ORDRE ROYAL DE VICTORIA MEMBRE QUATRIÈME CLASSE	**ORDER OF THE BRITISH EMPIRE (OFFICER)** / ORDRE DE L'EMPIRE BRITANNIQUE (OFFICIER)	**IMPERIAL SERVICE ORDER** / ORDRE DU SERVICE IMPÉRIAL	**ROYAL VICTORIAN ORDER MEMBER OF THE FIFTH CLASS** / ORDRE ROYAL DE VICTORIA MEMBRE CINQUIÈME CLASSE	**ORDER OF THE BRITISH EMPIRE (MEMBER)** / ORDRE DE L'EMPIRE BRITANNIQUE (MEMBRE)
MEDAL OF BRAVERY / MÉDAILLE DE LA BRAVOURE	**MEMBER OF THE ORDER OF CANADA** / MEMBRE DE L'ORDRE DU CANADA	**MEMBER OF THE ORDER OF MILITARY MERIT** / MEMBRE DE L'ORDRE DU MÉRITE MILITAIRE	**AIR FORCE CROSS** / CROIX DE L'AVIATION	**ROYAL RED CROSS (ASSOCIATE)** / CROIX-ROUGE ROYALE (ASSOCIÉ)	**ORDER OF SAINT JOHN** / ORDRE DE SAINT JEAN
DISTINGUISHED FLYING MEDAL / MÉDAILLE DU SERVICE DISTINGUÉ DANS L'AVIATION	**AIR FORCE MEDAL** / MÉDAILLE DE L'AVIATION	**BRITISH EMPIRE MEDAL** / MÉDAILLE DE L'EMPIRE BRITANNIQUE	**1939-45 STAR** / ÉTOILE DE 1939-1945	**ATLANTIC STAR** / ÉTOILE DE L'ATLANTIQUE	**AIR CREW EUROPE STAR** / ÉTOILE D'EUROPE SERVICE NAVIGUANT
CANADIAN VOLUNTEER SERVICE MEDAL / MÉDAILLE CANADIENNE DU VOLONTAIRE	**WAR MEDAL 1939-45** / MÉDAILLE DE LA GUERRE DE 1939-1945	**AFRICA SERVICE MEDAL OF THE UNION OF SOUTH AFRICA** / MEDAILLE DE L'UNION SUD AFRICAINE POUR SERVICE EN AFRIQUE	**INDIA SERVICE MEDAL** / MÉDAILLE DU SERVICE DE L'INDE	**NEW ZEALAND WAR SERVICE MEDAL** / MÉDAILLE DU SERVICE DE GUERRE DE NOUVELLE ZÉLANDE	**SOUTHERN RHODESIA SERVICE MEDAL** / MÉDAILLE DU SERVICE DE RHODÉSIE DU SUD
UNITED NATIONS MILITARY OBSERVATION GROUP IN INDIA AND PAKISTAN (UNMOGIP) / GROUPE D'OBSERVATEURS MILITAIRES DES NATIONS UNIES POUR L'INDE ET LE PAKISTAN (UNMOGIP)	**ORGANISATION DES NATIONS UNIES AU CONGO (ONUC)**	**UNITED NATIONS TEMPORARY EXECUTIVE AUTHORITY IN WEST NEW GUINEA (UNTEA)** / AUTORITÉ EXÉCUTIVE TEMPORAIRE DES NATIONS UNIES EN NOUVELLE-GUINÉE OCCIDENTALE (UNTEA)	**UNITED NATIONS YEMEN OBSERVATION MISSION (UNYOM)** / MISSION D'OBSERVATION DES NATIONS UNIES AU YÉMEN (UNYOM)	**UNITED NATIONS FORCE IN CYPRUS (UNFICYP)** / FORCE DES NATIONS UNIES A CHYPRE (UNFICYP)	**UNITED NATIONS INDIA PAKISTAN OBSERVATION MISSION (UNIPOM)** / MISSION D'OBSERVATION DES NATIONS UNIES POUR L'INDE ET LE PAKISTAN (UNIPOM)
KING GEORGE V JUBILEE MEDAL (1935) / MÉDAILLE DU JUBILÉ DU ROI GEORGE V (1935)	**KING GEORGE VI CORONATION MEDAL (1937)** / MÉDAILLE DU COURONNEMENT DU ROI GEORGE VI (1937)	**QUEEN ELIZABETH II CORONATION MEDAL (1953)** / MÉDAILLE DU COURONNEMENT DE LA REINE ELISABETH II (1953)	**CANADIAN CENTENNIAL MEDAL (1967)** / MÉDAILLE DU CENTENAIRE DU CANADA (1967)	**QUEEN ELIZABETH II JUBILEE MEDAL (1977)** / MÉDAILLE DU JUBILÉ DE LA REINE ELISABETH II (1977)	**ARMY LONG SERVICE AND GOOD CONDUCT MEDAL** / MÉDAILLE D'ANCIENNETÉ DE SERVICE ET DE BONNE CONDUITE ARMÉE
COLONIAL AUXILIARY FORCES LONG SERVICE MEDAL / MÉDAILLE D'ANCIENNETÉ DE SERVICE DANS LES FORCES AUXILIAIRES COLONIALES	**EFFICIENCY DECORATION (ED)** / DECORATION D'EFFICACITÉ (E D)	**EFFICIENCY MEDAL** / MÉDAILLE D'EFFICACITE	**DECORATION FOR OFFICERS OF THE NAVAL VOLUNTEER RESERVE (VRD)** / DECORATION POUR OFFICIERS DE LA RESERVE NAVALE VOLONTAIRE (V R D)	**NAVAL VOLUNTEER RESERVE LONG SERVICE AND GOOD CONDUCT MEDAL** / MÉDAILLE D'ANCIENNETÉ DE SERVICE ET DE BONNE CONDUITE RESERVE NAVALE VOLONTAIRE	**AIR EFFICIENCY AWARD** / INSIGNE D'EFFICACITÉ DANS L'AVIATION

FOOTNOTES

1. WHERE RIBBONS ARE REPEATED, IT IS TO SHOW THE DIFFERENT LEVELS AND THEIR ORDER OF PRECEDENCE. SEE CFAO 18-12 FOR FURTHER INFORMATION
2. A MAPLE LEAF ON THE CVSM INDICATES SERVICE OUTSIDE OF CANADA
3. OAK LEAF INDICATES "MENTIONED IN DISPATCHES" OR QUEEN'S COMMENDATION FOR BRAVE CONDUCT
4. A SILVER ROSETTE USUALLY DENOTES A SECOND AWARD OF A DECORATION OR MEDAL

5. A GOLD ROSETTE ON '39-45 STAR' AWARDED TO AIRCREWS OF FIGHTER AIRCRAFT ENGAGED IN BATTLE OF BRITAIN – 1 JULY TO 31 OCTOBER, 1940
6. AN 8, 1 OR ROSETTE MAY APPEAR ON THE AFRICA STAR
7. THE ORDER OF THE BRITISH EMPIRE AND THE B E M WHEN GIVEN FOR GALLANTRY, THE RIBBON BEARS CROSSED SILVER OAK LEAVES
8. ORDER OF ST JOHN – THE RIBBONS FOR COMMANDERS, OFFICERS, SERVING BROTHERS AND SISTERS ARE 1 1/2 INCHES WIDE FOR MEN 1 1/4 INCHES FOR WOMEN

DISPOSITION DES RUBANS DES ORDRES, DÉCORATIONS ET MÉDAILLES

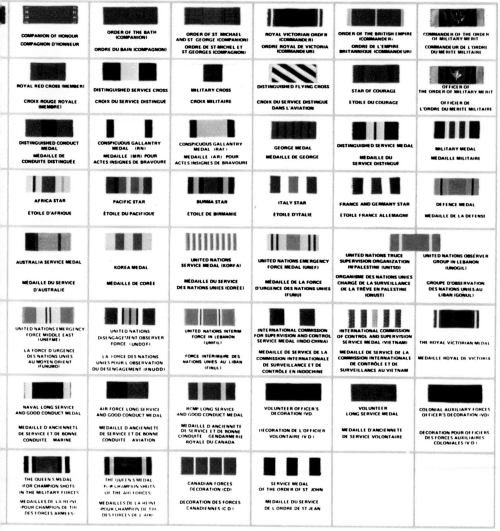

COMPANION OF HONOUR / COMPAGNON D'HONNEUR

ORDER OF THE BATH (COMPANION) / ORDRE DU BAIN (COMPAGNON)

ORDER OF ST MICHAEL AND ST GEORGE (COMPANION) / ORDRE DE ST MICHEL ET ST GEORGES (COMPAGNON)

ROYAL VICTORIAN ORDER (COMMANDER) / ORDRE ROYAL DE VICTORIA (COMMANDEUR)

ORDER OF THE BRITISH EMPIRE (COMMANDER) / ORDRE DE L'EMPIRE BRITANNIQUE (COMMANDEUR)

COMMANDER OF THE ORDER OF MILITARY MERIT / COMMANDEUR DE L'ORDRE DU MERITE MILITAIRE

ROYAL RED CROSS (MEMBER) / CROIX ROUGE ROYALE (MEMBRE)

DISTINGUISHED SERVICE CROSS / CROIX DU SERVICE DISTINGUÉ

MILITARY CROSS / CROIX MILITAIRE

DISTINGUISHED FLYING CROSS / CROIX DU SERVICE DISTINGUÉ DANS L'AVIATION

STAR OF COURAGE / ETOILE DU COURAGE

OFFICER OF THE ORDER OF MILITARY MERIT / OFFICIER DE L'ORDRE DU MERITE MILITAIRE

DISTINGUISHED CONDUCT MEDAL / MÉDAILLE DE CONDUITE DISTINGUÉE

CONSPICUOUS GALLANTRY MEDAL (RN) / MEDAILLE (MR) POUR ACTES INSIGNES DE BRAVOURE

CONSPICUOUS GALLANTRY MEDAL (RAF) / MEDAILLE (AR) POUR ACTES INSIGNES DE BRAVOURE

GEORGE MEDAL / MÉDAILLE DE GEORGE

DISTINGUISHED SERVICE MEDAL / MÉDAILLE DU SERVICE DISTINGUF

MILITARY MEDAL / MÉDAILLE MILITAIRE

AFRICA STAR / ÉTOILE D'AFRIQUE

PACIFIC STAR / ÉTOILE DU PACIFIQUE

BURMA STAR / ÉTOILE DE BIRMANIE

ITALY STAR / ÉTOILE D'ITALIE

FRANCE AND GERMANY STAR / ETOILE FRANCE ALLEMAGNE

DEFENCE MEDAL / MÉDAILLE DE LA DEFENSE

AUSTRALIA SERVICE MEDAL / MÉDAILLE DU SERVICE D'AUSTRALIE

KOREA MEDAL / MÉDAILLE DE CORÉE

UNITED NATIONS SERVICE MEDAL (KOREA) / MÉDAILLE DU SERVICE DES NATIONS UNIES (COREE)

UNITED NATIONS EMERGENCY FORCE MEDAL (UNEF) / MÉDAILLE DE LA FORCE D'URGENCE DES NATIONS UNIES (FUNU)

UNITED NATIONS TRUCE SUPERVISION ORGANIZATION IN PALESTINE (UNTSO) / ORGANISME DES NATIONS UNIES CHARGÉ DE LA SURVEILLANCE DE LA TRÊVE EN PALESTINE (ONUST)

UNITED NATIONS OBSERVER GROUP IN LEBANON (UNOGIL) / GROUPE D'OBSERVATION DES NATIONS UNIES AU LIBAN (GONUL)

UNITED NATIONS EMERGENCY FORCE MIDDLE EAST (UNEFME) / LA FORCE D'URGENCE DES NATIONS UNIES AU MOYEN ORIENT (FUNUMO)

UNITED NATIONS DISENGAGEMENT OBSERVER FORCE (UNDOF) / LA FORCE DES NATIONS UNIES POUR L'OBSERVATION DU DESENGAGEMENT (FNUOD)

UNITED NATIONS INTERIM FORCE IN LEBANON (UNIFIL) / FORCE INTÉRIMAIRE DES NATIONS UNIES AU LIBAN (FINUL)

INTERNATIONAL COMMISSION FOR SUPERVISION AND CONTROL SERVICE MEDAL (INDO-CHINA) / MÉDAILLE DE SERVICE DE LA COMMISSION INTERNATIONALE DE SURVEILLANCE ET DE CONTRÔLE EN INDOCHINE

INTERNATIONAL COMMISSION OF CONTROL AND SUPERVISION SERVICE MEDAL (VIETNAM) / MÉDAILLE DE SERVICE DE LA COMMISSION INTERNATIONALE DE CONTRÔLE ET DE SURVEILLANCE AU VIETNAM

THE ROYAL VICTORIAN MEDAL / MEDAILLE ROYAL DE VICTORIA

NAVAL LONG SERVICE AND GOOD CONDUCT MEDAL / MEDAILLE D'ANCIENNETE DE SERVICE ET DE BONNE CONDUITE MARINE

AIR FORCE LONG SERVICE AND GOOD CONDUCT MEDAL / MEDAILLE D'ANCIENNETE DE SERVICE ET DE BONNE CONDUITE AVIATION

RCMP LONG SERVICE AND GOOD CONDUCT MEDAL / MEDAILLE D'ANCIENNETE DE SERVICE ET DE BONNE CONDUITE GENDARMERIE ROYALE DU CANADA

VOLUNTEER OFFICER'S DECORATION (VD) / DÉCORATION DE L'OFFICIER VOLONTAIRE (VD)

VOLUNTEER LONG SERVICE MEDAL / MEDAILLE D'ANCIENNETE DE SERVICE VOLONTAIRE

COLONIAL AUXILIARY FORCES OFFICER'S DECORATION (VD) / DECORATION POUR OFFICIERS DES FORCES AUXILIAIRES COLONIALES (VD)

THE QUEEN'S MEDAL (FOR CHAMPION SHOTS IN THE MILITARY FORCES) / MEDAILLES DE LA REINE (POUR CHAMPION DE TIR DES FORCES ARMEES)

THE QUEEN'S MEDAL (FOR CHAMPION SHOTS OF THE AIR FORCES) / MEDAILLES DE LA REINE (POUR CHAMPION DE TIR DES FORCES DE L'AIR)

CANADIAN FORCES DECORATION (CD) / DECORATION DES FORCES CANADIENNES (CD)

SERVICE MEDAL OF THE ORDER OF ST JOHN / MEDAILLE DU SERVICE DE L'ORDRE DE ST JEAN

S'IL Y A PLUSIEURS RUBANS IDENTIQUES, C'EST POUR EN MONTRER LES DIVERS NIVEAUX ET ORDRE DE PRESEANCE VOIR L'OAFC 18 12 POUR DE PLUS AMPLES RENSEIGNEMENTS

UNE FEUILLE D'ERABLE SUR LA MÉDAILLE CANADIENNE DU VOLONTAIRE INDIQUE UNE PÉRIODE DE SERVICE À L'EXTÉRIEUR DU CANADA

UNE FEUILLE DE CHÊNE INDIQUE UNE "CITATION" OU UN "ÉLOGE DE LA REINE" POUR BRAVOURE

UNE ROSETTE ARGENTÉE INDIQUE HABITUELLEMENT UNE DEUXIÈME REMISE D'UNE MÊME DÉCORATION OU MÉDAILLE

5 UNE ROSETTE DORÉE SUR UNE ÉTOILE DE 1939 1945 EST DÉCERNÉE AUX ÉQUIPAGES AÉRIENS DES AÉRONEFS QUI ONT PARTICIPÉ À LA BATAILLE DE GRANDE BRETAGNE DU 1ᵉʳ JUILLET AU 31 OCTOBRE 1940

6 LE CHIFFRE 8 OU 1 UNE ROSETTE PEUT PARAÎTRE SUR L'ÉTOILE D'AFRIQUE

7 SI L'ORDRE DE L'EMPIRE BRITANNIQUE ET LA MÉDAILLE DE L'EMPIRE BRITANNIQUE SONT DÉCERNÉS POUR GALANTERIE, LE GALON PORTERA DES FEUILLES DE CHÊNE ARGENTÉES ENTRECROISÉS

8 L'ORDRE DE ST JEAN - LA LARGEUR DES GALONS DES COMMANDEURS, OFFICIERS ET DE FRÈRES ET SOEURS SERVANTS EST 1 1/2 PO POUR LES HOMMES 1 1/4 POUR LES FEMMES

DC AUG 1981
DC Août 1981